GARDENS OF SCOTLAND 2007

Contents

FRONT COVER

by

Paul Carline

Printed by Inglis Allen, 40 Townsend Place, Kirkcaldy, Fife.

SCOTLAND'S GARDENS SCHEME

Created as a registered charity in 1931 Scotland's Gardens Scheme's objective was to raise funds for the Queen's Nurses, a charity that supported community nurses in primary care, by opening country house gardens to the public for a nominal charge.

Today Scotland's Gardens Scheme has a small management team and approximately two hundred volunteers in twenty-seven Scottish districts who organise the opening of an average of three hundren and fifty, mostly private, gardens to the public, ranging from formal castle gardens to groups of small village gardens.

The Queen's Nursing Institute Scotland (as it has become) remains one of the Scheme's principal beneficiaries' the other is the Garden's Fund of the National Trust for Scotland. Perennial (The Gardener's Royal Benevolent Society) and The Royal Fund for Gardeners' Children also receive support annually. These four worthy charities receive 60% (net.) of the money raised from the garden openings whilst 40% (gross) is allocated to charities of the garden owner's choice.

Most garden openings provide home-baked teas and a plant stall. At some there are other attractions and stalls. Children accompanied by adults are welcome.

In 2006/7 a total of £162,907 was distributed to charities. In addition to the four SGS beneficiaries 176 other registered charities nominated by garden owners were supported

CHAIRMAN'S MESSAGE

At the beginning of my time as Chairman, I would like first of all to take my hat off to both Charlotte Hunt, Chairman for the last five years, and of course Robin St. Clair-Ford who has been Director for twenty-four years! They can both take a great deal of credit for SGS being where it is now.

A little alarming for both Paddy Scott, the new Director, and me to be arriving with our shiny new faces at the same moment. There are things which we will have to try hard to keep up to speed on, but at the same time there is a feeling of a new paintbrush wielded by different artists and therefore a fresh look at lots of things.

The marketing side of this business, for it has become a business, is paramount and I hope that many networking fingers will be activated to inspire more people to visit our wonderful gardens opening for charity this year.

The importance of the private gardens that open for us on one or more days, whether large gardens, town gardens or groups of tiny village gardens cannot be underestimated. They are our backbone. Happily, we are also supported by many 'ever open' gardens giving us a donation and most of the gardens of the National Trust for Scotland open for us on specific days. Furthermore, we are truly fortunate to have an outstanding group of people who keep all the wheels turning - District Organisers, Area Organisers, Treasurers, Garden Owners, Gardeners, Tea Ladies. The list could go on and on, but thank you all for everything you do.

THE QUEEN'S NURSING INSTITUTE SCOTLAND

Patron: Her Majesty The Queen

31 Castle Terrace, Edinburgh, EH1 2EL

Tel 0131 229 2333 Fax 0131 2289066

Registered Charity no SC005751

Brief History of QNIS

In 1887 Queen Victoria set aside £70,000 from her Jubilee Gift Fund to improve the nursing care of the sick and poor. Two years later saw the foundation by Royal Charter of the QNI. Training centres were established and nurses gained the skills and the knowledge necessary to care for people in the community.

In time, throughout the country every village and district had its own nurse, respected and loved: affectionately known as "The Jubilee Nurse".

> **Originally the concept of Scotland's Gardens Scheme was to contribute to the training and pensions of the Queen's Nurses.**

In 1948 the National Health Service assumed responsibility for funding the training of district nurses, but it was not until 1970 that this training was fully integrated into the National Health Service. Since 1970 the QNIS has worked to support and promote all that is excellent in community nursing.

The Present

QNIS is governed by Council and the day to day business managed by the Nurse Director with the help of a small dedicated administrative team. The work is wide and varied:

- Provision of educational grants and research fellowships

> **"As a mother with five children I would have found it extremely hard to train as a Public Health Nurse without your support. I was so happy I thought I had won the lottery."**
>
> Angela Gray, Brigid Stewart Scholarship Award 2005

- Organises conferences and workshops throughout Scotland
- Influences decision making in the best interests of nurses and the communities they serve (at local and national level)

The QNIS is indebted to SGS for the generous donation it receives, enabling many projects to proceed, all of them meeting unmet needs within the community.

- Funding of innovative Community Nursing Projects.

  Each application for funding of a project is given serious consideration by an independent QNIS committee to ensure sound management and ability to deliver.

  Examples of such projects include:

  o Healthy Outer Hebrideans, Western Isles Family Health nurses are developing a project to improve men's health. An opportunity will be provided for the men working in small businesses and industry on the island to receive a comprehensive health check.

  o Structured Diabetes Education Programme There is a general increase in the number of people suffering from diabetes. This project in Lanarkshire will provide group sessions for people newly diagnosed. Those attending will learn more about their medical condition in a non threatening friendly environment. With new knowledge and confidence the group of patients will be encouraged to take ownership of this long term condition and provide mutual support.

  o Community of Practice for the Development of Minor Illness The management of minor illnesses is a new role for both practice and district nurses. The Community of Practice, of nurses who have completed modules on this topic, is about to be established in Glasgow. A facilitator will enable the group to focus on developing statements of good practice to share with colleagues new to the role.

  o Hungry for Health A community children's nurse working in partnership with schools in the Cowal Peninsula aims to roll out the Hungry for Health Award Scheme. Children age 7-11 years will have the opportunity to achieve this award by demonstrating a healthy lifestyle that includes physical activity, healthy eating, oral hygiene and mental health.

  o MY Group This project is an innovative partnership in Millport, Isle of Cumbrae, between community based nurses and the police. The youth group aims to reduce alcohol consumption and related health problems by provision of alternative activities such as sport, health and beauty therapy.

  o Nocturia Many older people experience interrupted sleep due to the need to visit the bathroom several times a night. This study will examine the factors involved, including the added risk of trips and falls and subsequent hospitalisation.

- Fellowship of QNIS- available to nurses who demonstrate excellence and leadership.

> **"I have gained more confidence to be a better leader and manager. I have proved to myself that I am a good nurse and I have the confidence to study at a higher level."**
>
> Pauline Waugh Fellowship by Assessment 2006

- Ensures effective communication with community nurses throughout Scotland.

- The welfare of retired Queen's nurses is a further key aspect of the work of QNIS in remembering those who have given so much of their time and effort to the community. Pensions, visiting scheme, special grants, group holidays, newsletter and annual gatherings.

Changing times and the future

Perhaps change is the one constant we can rely on, particularly in relation to the Health Service. The pace of change is challenging. Some of the influencing factors necessitating change can be summarised as follows:

- Ensuring all groups have equal access to nursing services and do not suffer disadvantage.

- Increase in gap between rich and poor.

- Recurrence of old, and increase of new diseases (tuberculosis HIV, AIDS, Hepatitis C)

- Challenges of obesity, lack of exercise, mental health problems in children.

- Technological advances

- Ever increasing diagnostic aids for acute and long term conditions

- Rising expectations of the NHS

- The need for a robust evidence base for nursing and medicine.

- Demographic changes (increasing numbers of older people with complex health conditions).

- Diminishing numbers of work age adults with resultant implications for recruitment.

Understandably the NHS struggles and 'juggles' to set priorities, allocate resources, as well as obtain best value for money- inevitably a quart into a pint pot. Quite simply demand always exceeds capacity to supply. A recent review of Community Nursing in Scotland has highlighted "the challenges nurses face in community settings today are very different from those of their predecessors. More difficult still will be the challenges faced by tomorrow's nurses."

> "...more difficult still will be the challenges faced by tomorrow's nurses"
>
> Review of Nursing in the Community 2006

'Gardening for Health'

We were delighted to participate in the 76th birthday celebrations of Scotland's Gardens Scheme by holding a competition, 'Gardening for Health'. This seemed an appropriate and fitting way to mark our longstanding relationship. Competition leaflets were circulated widely to hospitals, hospices and residential care home throughout Scotland. The underlying principle of the competition was simple: 'Do you have an area or garden that would benefit people with a health problem, that you would like to create or improve? Tell us what you would plan to do to increase the enjoyment to suit the needs of your patients, residents and visitors'.

We received a considerable number of high quality applications. In some instances patients/residents had been involved in the design and the application process.

The chairman and Director of Scotland's Gardens Scheme kindly assisted in selecting the winners, carefully considering, range and number of people to benefit from improvements, planning proposals that would take into account sight, smell, taste, sound, colour and how realistic the proposal was to achieve.

We were delighted to welcome representatives and their poster presentations to the QNIS AGM

Finally, a very big thank you to SGS, District Organisers, Garden Owners and the visiting public for your continued support.

The National Trust for Scotland

There is something wonderfully symbolic about the fact that both Scotland's Gardens Scheme and The National Trust for Scotland have been celebrating their 75th birthday during 2006. From the beginning there has been a commonality of interest and many significant personalities who have given their commitment, knowledge and enthusiasm to both organisations, or have recognised that – so far as Scotland's gardens are concerned – the purposes of the two organisations are entirely complementary. We enjoyed a wonderful day together at Threave on 30 May when HRH The Duke of Rothesay, Patron of the NTS, and HRH The Duchess of Rothesay, Patron of SGS, graced us with their presence and placed a seal on our shared anniversaries. It was so obvious that they shared our love of gardens, and indeed the garden at Highgrove has become known as one of the great British gardens of the late twentieth century.

An often neglected fact is that Scotland's gardens produce *food*, food which lays the lightest possible imprint upon the earth, celebrates the fact that Scotland is a country of infinite variety and local-ness, in its garden culture as much as in its building culture, and that some of the most delicious fruits and vegetables consumed in Britain's restaurants comes from Scotland.

As in Scotland's gardens generally, 2006 has been a 'good growing year'. There have been long summer days, and the warm weather has resulted in bumper crops of fruit and vegetables, and our 'Apple Days' had plenty of varieties to be viewed, identified and sampled. Autumn colours came late but hung on despite the odd gale, with some spectacular colour in both gardens and countryside well into November. Concerns continue that our climate is clearly changing and, amazingly, autumn saw many rhododendrons with a heavy second flowering that did not bode well for those particular plants or, more widely, our environment.

The Trust is currently working both to assess and to improve the environmental impact of our gardening activities. I have personally, as Chairman of the Trust, taken on the chairmanship of the implementation group that is working to make a reality of our 2005 *Environmental Policy*. I believe that, if Scotland's Gardens Scheme and the Trust could put their shoulders jointly to the wheel, we could together make an immense difference to the wise stewardship of our energy resources, promote organic gardening and such simple but highly effective techniques such as 'companion planting', and provide a real witness to the effectiveness of measures which would place Scotland in the forefront of responsible nations.

There are many good things going on in our gardens: Canna House, on the island of Canna, is to have a gardener again after many years and the laird's garden will flourish and become fruitful again; the Conservation Management Plan for the *Revival of the Gardens & Designed Landscape of Newhailes* has just been completed and will, we hope, make Newhailes with its unique 18th century survivals something akin to The Lost Gardens of Heligan in its fruitfulness and attractiveness as a place to visit and enjoy. In terms of design, we were delighted that our *Garden of Scottish Fruits* at Fyvie Castle, designed by Robert Grant, has received one of Aberdeenshire County Council's well merited design awards.

However, all these good things could hardly be achieved without partnership, and especially partnerships between our two characteristically Scottish organisations that are even coeval in date. May that partnership grow and flourish, and our heartfelt thanks for the support which we receive from you, one of our greatest partners and supporters.

SHONAIG MACPHERSON
Chairman, The National Trust for Scotland

THE ROYAL FUND FOR GARDENERS' CHILDREN

Registered Charity No: 248746

Our Fund has been helping the orphaned children of professional horticulturists since 1887. We can also offer support to needy children, whose parents are employed in horticulture, and with this very much in mind, the decision was taken this year to change our name from the original Royal Gardeners' Orphan Fund to The Royal Fund for Gardeners' Children. We trust that the new, more inclusive, name better reflects the help we are able to give to all gardeners' children, not just those who have been orphaned

In total this year we have helped seventy-seven children, twenty-six of whom have lost a parent. In Scotland we have been helping two orphaned children on a regular basis and have helped a further twelve with the provision of such items as winter clothing, school uniform, bedding and a much needed family holiday.

The support we receive from Scotland's Gardens Scheme is very important to the work we undertake in Scotland and we are glad to have this opportunity to express our appreciation.

If you would like further information regarding our work, or to advise of any children who may qualify for our help please contact our Secretary:-

Mrs Kate Wallis

10 Deards Wood, Knebworth, Herts SG3 6PG

Tel/Fax: 01438 813939 email: rfgc@btinternet.com

PERENNIAL
GARDENERS' ROYAL BENEVOLENT SOCIETY
Helping Horticulturists In Need Since 1839

Sometimes, horticulturists require as much care as the gardens in this book.

Perennial - Gardeners' Royal Benevolent Society the only charity dedicated to helping Scottish horticulturists in need.
We offer care, advice and support for horticulturists throughout their lives, as we have been doing since 1839. We are grateful for the support of all garden owners participating in Scotland's Gardens Scheme.

For further information on Perennial, or how your donation will make a difference, please telephone 01372 373962 or visit our website, www.perennial.org.uk/scotland.

An exempt charity no.15408R

Scotland's Gardens Scheme
Gardens open for charity

We welcome gardens large and small and also groups of gardens. If you would like information on how to open your garden for charity please contact us at the address below.

SCOTLAND'S GARDENS SCHEME,
42a CASTLE STREET, EDINBURGH EH2 3BN
Telephone: 0131 226 3714
E-mail: info@sgsgardens.co.uk
Website: www.gardensofscotland

✂ ....

NAME & ADDRESS: (Block capitals please)

....

....

....

Postcode.................................. Tel:...

E-mail..

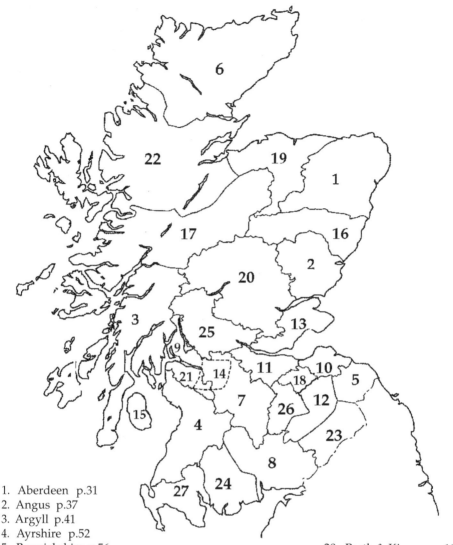

Gardens Open on a Regular Basis or By Appointment

Full details are given in the District List of Gardens

ABERDEEN

23 Don Street, Old Aberdeen	July by appointment
Blairwood, Aberdeen	Mid June - beginning Oct. by appointment
Grandhome, Aberdeen	By appointment
Greenridge, Cults	July & August by appointment
Hatton Castle, Turriff	By appointment
Howemill, Craigievar	By appointment
Kildrummy Castle Gardens, Alford	April - October daily
Lochan House, Black Chambers	Groups by appointment
Ploughman's Hall, Old Rayne	By appointment

ANGUS

House of Pitmuies, Guthrie, by Forfar	1 April - 31 October 10am - 5pm
Melgam House, Lintrathen, Kirriemuir	1 April - 30 September 9am - dusk

ARGYLL

Achnacloich, Connel	8 April - 31 October daily 10am - 6pm
An Cala, Ellenabeich	1 April - 31 October daily 10am - 6pm
Ardchattan Priory, North Connel.	1 April - 31 October daily 9am - 6pm
Ardkinglas Woodland Garden	All year daily - daylight hours
Ardmaddy Castle, by Oban	All year daily 9am - sunset or by appt.
Ardno, Cairndow	By appointment
Ascog Hall, Isle of Bute	Easter - End Oct Weds - Suns 10am - 5pm
Barguillean's "Angus Garden"	All year daily 9am - 6pm
Cnoc-na-Garrie, Ballymeanoch	By appointment
Druimavuic House, Appin	April, May & June daily 10am - 6pm
Druimneil House, Port Appin	1 April - 31 October daily 9am - 6pm
Eckford, By Dunoon	9 April - 6 June daily 10am - 5pm
Glecknabae, Isle of Bute	Spring - Autumn by appointment
Jura House, Ardfin, Isle of Jura.	All year 9am - 5pm
Kildalloig, Campbeltown	By appointment
Kinlochlaich House Gardens, Appin.	All year 9.30 -5.30 or dusk (except Suns Oct - Mar) also Suns Apr - Sept 10.30am - 5.30pm
Torosay Castle Gardens, Isle of Mull	All year

13

BERWICKSHIRE

Bughtrig, Leitholm .... 1 June – 1 September daily 11am – 5pm

Netherbyres, Eyemouth .... By appointment (for parties 10 or over)

CAITHNESS, SUTHERLAND & ORKNEY

Kerrachar, Kylesku .... Mid May - mid Sept Tues, Thurs & Suns
and by appointment

Langwell, Berriedale .... By appointment

CLYDESDALE

Baitlaws, Lamington .... June, July, August by appointment

Carmichael Mill, Lanark .... By appointment

DUNBARTONSHIRE WEST

Glenarn, Rhu .... Daily 21 March - 21 Sept. sunrise - sunset

EAST LOTHIAN

Inwood, Carberry .... 1 Apr. - 30 Sept. Tues, Thurs, & Sats 2 - 5pm
Also groups by appointment

Shepherd House, Inveresk .... 17 April - 28 June Tues & Thurs 2 - 4pm
Also groups by appointment

Stobshiel House, Humbie .... By appointment

EDINBURGH & WEST LOTHIAN

61 Fountainhall Road, Edinburgh .... By appointment

Newliston, Kirkliston .... 2 May - 3 June Wed - Sun 2 - 6pm

FIFE

Barham, Bow of Fife .... 15 February - 30 September by appointment

Cambo House, Kingsbarns .... All year 10am - 5pm

Strathtyrum, St Andrews .... June, Aug. & Sept. Weds. - Suns 2 - 4pm

GLASGOW

Invermay, Cambuslang .... April - September by appointment

KINCARDINE & DEESIDE

4 Robert Street, Stonehaven .... 1 July - 31 July by appointment

LOCHABER, BADENOCH & STRATHSPEY

Ardtornish, Lochaline, Morvern .... *1 April - 31 October 10am - 6pm*

MIDLOTHIAN

Newhall, Carlops .... *By arrangement*
The Old Sun Inn, Newhall .... *1 May - 29 July most days by appointment*

MORAY & NAIRN

Knocknagore, Knockando .... *By appointment*

PERTH & KINROSS

Ardvorlich, Lochearnhead .... *6 May to 3 June all day*
Bolfracks, Aberfeldy .... *1 April - 31October 10am - 6pm*
Braco Castle, Braco .... *1 February - 31 October 10am - 5pm*
Cluniemore, Pitlochry .... *1 May - 1 Oct by appointment*
Cluny House, Aberfeldy .... *1 March - 31 October 10am - 6pm*
Dowhill, Cleish .... *April & June Thursdays 1 - 4pm*
Drummond Castle .... *May - October daily 2 - 6pm*
Easter Meikle Fardle, Meikleour .... *May - mid August by appointment*
Glendoick, by Perth .... *9 April - 8 June Mon - Fri 10am - 4pm*
Rossie House, Forgandenny .... *1 March - 31 October by appointment*
Scone Palace, Perth .... *1 April - 31 October 9.30am - 5.30pm*
Strathgarry House, Killiecrankie .... *June, July, August by appointment*
The Bank House, Glenfarg .... *Mid May - 31 August by appointment*
Wester Dalqueich, Carnbo .... *May - 31 August by appointment*

ROSS, CROMARTY, SKYE & INVERNESS

Abriachan, Loch Ness Side .... *February - November 9am - dusk*
An Acarsaid, Ord, Sleat, Isle of Skye .... *April - October 10am - 5.30pm*
Attadale, Strathcarron .... *1 Apr-end Oct (Closed Suns) 10am - 5.30pm*
Balmeanach House, Struan .... *Weds & Sats end Apr - mid Oct 11am - 4.30pm*
Coiltie Garden, Divach, Drumnadrochit . *20 June - 20 July daily noon - 7pm*
Dunvegan Castle, Isle of Skye .... *Mid March - 31 Oct. daily 10am - 5.30pm*
1 Nov. - Mid March daily 11am - 4pm
Leathad Ard, Isle of Lewis .... *9 June - 23 August Tues, Thurs, Sats 2 - 6pm*
Leckmelm Shrubbery & Arboretum .... *1 April - 31 October daily 10am - 6pm*

ROXBURGH

Floors Castle, Kelso .... *All year daily 9.30am - 5pm*

Monteviot, Jedburgh .... *1 April - 31 October daily 12 - 5pm*

STEWARTRY OF KIRKCUDBRIGHT
Arndarroch, St John's Town of Dalry .... *July - September by appointment*
Barnhourie Mill, Colvend .... *May - October by appointment*
Cally Gardens, Gatehouse of Fleet .... *7 April - 30 September, Tues - Fri 2 - 5.30pm,*
Sat & Sun 10am - 5.30pm
Carleton Croft, Borgue .... *July - August by appointment*
Corsock House, Castle Douglas .... *Apr. - June by appt. (and for autumn colours)*
Danevale Park, Crossmichael .... *To 1 June by appointment*
Southwick House, Dumfries .... *Monday 25 - Friday 29 June*

STIRLING
14 Glebe Crescent, Tillicoultry .... *By appointment*
Arndean, Stirling .... *By appointment mid May - end June*
Callander Lodge, Callander .... *April - end August by appointment*
Culbuie, Buchlyvie .... *May - Oct. Tues. 1 - 5pm & groups by appt.*
Gargunnock House, Gargunnock .... *Feb - 11 March, Sun/Weds 10.30am - 3.30pm,*
April - mid June, Sept./Oct. 2 - 5pm
Kilbryde Castle, Dunblane .... *By appointment*
Milseybank, Bridge of Allan .... *By appointment*
The Steading, Hillhead .... *Groups by appointment*
Thorntree, Arnprior .... *By appointment*

TWEEDDALE
Kailzie Gardens, Peebles .... *All year 10am - 5.30pm*
Portmore, Eddleston .... *June, July, August by appointment*

WIGTOWN
Ardwell House Gardens, Ardwell .... *1 April - 30 September daily 10am - 5pm*
Castle Kennedy & Lochinch, Stranraer ..... *Sundays 4 Feb - 11 March 10am - 5pm*
1 April - 30 September daily 10am - 5pm
Glenwhan Gardens, by Stranraer .... *1 April - 31 October daily 10am - 5pm*
Logan House Gardens, Port Logan .... *2 February - 1 April 9am - 6pm*
2 April - 31 August 9am - 6pm
Woodfall Gardens, Glasserton .... *May -31 August by appointment*

MONTHLY LIST
Full details are given in the District List of Gardens

To be announced
Edinburgh & West Lothian .... Dalmeny Park, South Queensferry

Saturday 10 February
Roxburgh .... Mertoun Gardens, St Boswells

Sunday 11 February
Roxburgh .... Mertoun Gardens, St Boswells
Wigtown .... Kirkdale, Carsluith

Thursday 15 February
Roxburgh .... Floors Castle, Kelso

Sunday 18 February
Renfrew & Inverclyde .... Ardgowan, Inverkip
Stewartry of Kirkcudbright .... Danevale Park, Crossmichael
Wigtown .... Kirkdale, Carsluith

Sunday 25 February
Ayrshire .... Blairquhan, Straiton
Renfrew & Inverclyde .... Auchengrange & Lochside,
                                                    Lochwinnoch

Sunday 1 April
East Lothian .... Winton House, Pencaitland
Renfrew & Inverclyde .... Finlaystone, Langbank

Sunday 8 April
Edinburgh & West Lothian .... 61 Fountainhall Road, Edinburgh

Saturday 14 April
Ross, Cromarty, Skye & Inverness .. .. Inverewe, Poolewe

Sunday 15 April
Edinburgh & West Lothian .... 61 Fountainhall Road, Edinburgh
Midlothian .... Oxenfoord Castle, near Pathhead
Perth & Kinross .... Megginch Castle, Errol
Stirling .... Milseybank, Bridge of Allan

Sunday 22 April
Argyll .... Benmore Botanic Garden, Dunoon
Dunbartonshire West .... Kilarden, Rosneath
Ettrick & Lauderdale .... Bemersyde, Melrose

| Moray & Nairn | Knocknagore, Knockando |
| Stirling | Auchmar, Drymen |

Thursday 26 April

| Ross, Cromarty, Skye & Inverness | Dundonnell House, Wester Ross |

Sunday 29 April

| Fife | Cambo House, Kingsbarns |
| Stirling | The Pass House, Kilmahog, Callander |

Saturday 5 May

| Argyll | Arduaine, Kilmelford |

Sunday 6 May

Argyll	Arduaine, Kilmelford
Dumfries	Portrack House, Holywood
Perth & Kinross	Branklyn, Perth
Perth & Kinross	Glendoick, by Perth
Stewartry of Kirkcudbright	Walton Park, Castle Douglas
Wigtown	Logan House Gardens, Port Logan

Saturday 12 May

| Argyll | Knock Cottage, Lochgair |

Sunday 13 May

Angus	Brechin Castle, Brechin
Argyll	Crinan Hotel Garden, Crinan
Argyll	Knock Cottage, Lochgair
Argyll	Minard Castle, Minard
Dunbartonshire West	Geilston Garden, Cardross
East Lothian	Shepherd House, Inveresk
East Lothian	Tyninghame House, Dunbar
Edinburgh & West Lothian	Dean Gardens, Edinburgh
Glasgow & District	122 Millersneuk Crescent, Millerston
Renfrew & Inverclyde	Kilmacolm
Ross, Cromarty, Skye & Inverness	Kilcoy Castle, Muir of Ord
Stirling	Kilbryde Castle, Dunblane

Saturday 19 May

Argyll	Colintraive Gardens
Argyll	Kilbrandon, Balvicar
Argyl	Knock Cottage, Lochgair

Sunday 20 May

Angus	Dalfruin, Kirktonhill Road, Kirriemuir
Angus	Dunninald, Montrose
Argyll	Colintraive Gardens

Argyll	Duachy, Kilninver
Argyll	Kilbrandon, Balvicar
Argyll	Knock Cottage, Lochgair
Ayrshire	Kirkhill Castle
Berwickshire	Charterhall, Duns
Dunbartonshire West	Ross Priory, Gartocharn
East Lothian	Clint, Stenton, nr. Dunbar
Edinburgh & West Lothian	61 Fountainhall Road, Edinburgh
Glasgow & District	Kilsyth Gardens
Lochaber, Badenoch & Strathspey	Ard-Daraich, Ardgour, by Fort William
Perth & Kinross	Glendoick, by Perth
Stewartry of Kirkcudbright	Danevale Park, Crossmichael
Stirling	Gargunnock House, Gargunnock
Stirling	Yellowcraig Wood, Stirling District
Wigtown,	Lochryan House, Stranraer

Saturday 26 May

Argyll	Strachur House Flower & Woodland Gardens

Sunday 27 May

Argyll	Strachur House Flower & Woodland Gardens
Ayrshire	Doonholm, Ayr
East Lothian	Greywalls Hotel, Gullane
Edinburgh & West Lothian	61 Fountainhall Road, Edinburgh
Edinburgh & West Lothian	Suntrap, Gogarbank, Edinburgh
Fife	Saline Village Gardens, Saline
Kincardine & Deeside	Inchmarlo House Garden, Banchory
Lochaber, Badenoch & Strathspey	Aberarder, Kinlochlaggan
Lochaber, Badenoch & Strathspey	Ardverikie, Kinlochlaggan
Midlothian	Penicuik House, Penicuik
Perth & Kinross	Fingask Castle, Rait
Stewarty of Kirkcudbright	Corsock House, Castle Douglas
Stirling	Lochdochart, Crianlarich
Stirling	Touch
Tweeddale	Baddinsgill, West Linton
Wigtown	Logan Botanic Garden, Port Logan

Wednesday 30 May

Ross, Cromarty, Skye & Inverness	House of Gruinard, Laide

Saturday 2 June

Ross, Cromarty, Skye & Inverness	Attadale, Strathcarron

Sunday 3 June

Aberdeen	Dunecht House Gardens, Dunecht
Aberdeen	Kildrummy Castle Gardens, Alford

Angus .... Cortachy Castle, Kirriemuir
Berwickshire .... Whitchester House, Duns
Dumfries, ... Dalswinton House
Dunbartonshire West .... East Bay Gardens, Helensburgh
East Lothian .... Athelstaneford Village
Fife .... Earlshall Castle, Leuchars
Fife .... Micklegarth, Aberlour
Glasgow & District .... 44 Gordon Road, Netherlee
Kincardine & Deeside .... The Burn House & The Burn Garden
                                                                            House, Glenesk
Moray & Nairn .... Woodlands, Nairn
Perth & Kinross .... Delvine, Spittalfield
Renfrew & Inverclyde .... Carruth, Bridge of Weir
Stirling .... Duntreath Castle, Blanefield
Tweeddale .... Hallmanor, Kirkton Manor, Peebles

Thursday 7 June
Ross, Cromarty, Skye & Inverness .... Dundonnell House, Wester Ross

Saturday 9 June
Argyll .... Crarae Garden, Inveraray
Caithness & Sutherland .... Amat, Ardgay
Edinburgh & West Lothian .... Sawmill, Harburn
Ross, Cromarty, Skye & Inverness .... Brahan, Dingwall

Sunday 10 June
Aberdeen .... Esslemont, Ellon
Aberdeen .... Tillypronie, Tarland
Argyll .... Crarae Garden, Inveraray
Caithness & Sutherland .... Amat, Ardgay
Clydesdale .... Lamington Village & Overburns,
                                                                            Lamington
Clydesdale .... Nemphlar Village Garden Trail,
                                                                            Nemphlar, Lanark
Dunbartonshire West .... Cardross Gardens, Cardross
East Lothian .... Aberlady Village Gardens
Edinburgh & West Lothian .... Moray Place & Bank Gardens,
                                                                            Edinburgh
Fife .... Arnot Tower & Greenhead of Arnot
Fife .... Aytounhill House, Newburgh
Moray & Nairn .... Carestown Steading
Perth & Kinross .... Comrie Village Gardens, Comrie
Ross, Cromarty, Skye & Inverness .... Novar, Evanton
Stewartry of Kirkcudbright .... Cally Gardens, Gatehouse of Fleet
Stirling .... Kilbryde Castle, Dunblane
Stirling .... The Steading, Hillhead
Wigtown .... Woodfall Gardens, Glasserton

Saturday 16 June

Argyll	Achnacille, Kilmelford, by Oban
Midlothian	Lasswade: 16 Kevock Road

Sunday 17 June

Argyll	Achnacille, Kilmelford, by Oban
Ayrshire	Blair House, Dalry
Clydesdale	Dippoolbank Cottage, Carnwath
East Lothian	Gifford Bank with Broadwoodside Gifford
Midlothian	Lasswade: 16 Kevock Road
Moray & Nairn	Bents Green, 10 Pilmuir Rd. W, Forres
Perth & Kinross	Bradystone House, Murthly
Perth & Kinross	Explorers: The Scottish Plant Hunters Garden
Renfrew & Inverclyde	Bridge of Weir Gardens
Roxburgh	Smailholm Village Gardens
Stewartry of Kirkcudbright	The Old Manse, Crossmichael
Stirling	Plaka & other Bridge of Allan Gardens Pendreich Road, Bridge of Allan

Sunday 24 June

Aberdeen	Howemill, Craigievar
Angus	Newtonmill House, by Edzell
Argyll	Glecknabae, Rothesay
Ayrshire	Ladyburn, by Maybole
Berwickshire	Antons Hill, Leitholm
Clydesdale	20 Smithcroft, Hamilton
Dunbartonshire West	Queen Street Gardens, Helensburgh
East Lothian	Tyninghame House, Dunbar
Fife	Aytounhill House, Newburgh
Fife	Kirklands, Saline
Kincardine & Deeside	Crathes Castle, Banchory
Perth & Kinross	Blair Castle Gardens, Blair, Atholl
Perth & Kinross	Cleish Gardens, Cleish
Renfrew & Inverclyde	Houston Gardens
Ross, Cromarty, Skye & Inverness	House of Aigas and Field Centre, by Beauly
Stewartry of Kirkcudbright	Southwick House, Southwick
Stirling	Cambusmore & other Callander Gardens
Wigtown	Glenwhan Gardens, by Stranraer

Saturday 30 June

Caithness & Sutherland	Dunrobin Castle & Gardens, Golspie
Renfrew & Inverclyde	Sma' Shot Cottages Heritage Centre

Sunday 1 July

Aberdeen	Ploughman's Hall, Old Rayne
Angus	Edzell Village
Ayrshire	Penkill Castle
Dumfries	Cowhill Tower, Holywood
East Lothian	Stevenson House and the Walled Garden, Stevenson
Fife	Aytounhill House, Newburgh
Fife	Balcarres, Colinsburgh
Fife	Myres Castle, Auchtermuchty
Isle of Aran	Dougarie
Midlothian	Newhall, Carlops
Perth & Kinross	Carig Dhubh, Bonskeid
Perth & Kinross	Strathgarry House, Killiecrankie
Ross, Cromarty, Skye & Inverness	Kilcoy Castle, Muir of Ord
Stewartry of Kirkcudbright	Broughton House Garden, Kirkcudbright
Wigtown	Craichlaw, Kirkcowan

Saturday 7 July

Edinburgh & West Lothian	Malleny Garden, Balerno
Roxburgh	Floors Castle, Kelso

Sunday 8 July

Aberdeen	23 Don Street, Old Aberdeen
Angus	Gallery, Montrose
Berwickshire	Netherbyres, Eyemouth
Clydesdale	Wyndales Cottage, Symington
Dumfries	Dabton, Thornhill
Edinburgh & West Lothian	36 Morningside Drive, Edinburgh
Ettrick & Lauderdale	Fairnilee House, Torquhan
Fife	Earlshall Castle, Leuchars
Kincardine & Deeside	Findrack, Torphins
Perth & Kinross	Comrie Village Gardens, Comrie
Roxburgh	Gardens in Buccleuch Chase, St Boswells
Roxburgh	Floors Castle, Kelso
Stewartry of Kirkcudbright	Threave Garden, Castle Douglas
Stirling	Southwood, Stirling
Wigtown	Castle Kennedy & Lochinch Gardens, Stranraer

Wednesday 11 July

Caithness & Sutherland	Castle & Gardens of Mey, Caithness
Roxburgh	The Ask Organic Garden, Jedburgh

Saturday 14 July

Edinburgh & West Lothian	9 Braid Farm Road, Edinburgh
Ettrick & Lauderdale	Carolside, Earlston

Sunday 15 July

Angus	Glamis Castle, Glamis
Ayrshire	Knockdolian, Colmonell
Clydesdale	Biggar Park, Biggar
East Lothian	Inwood, Carberry
Edinburgh & West Lothian	9 Braid Farm Road, Edinburgh
Edinburgh & West Lothian	15 Morningside Park, Edinburgh
Fife	Wormistoune, Crail
Isle of Arran	Brodick Castle & Country Park
Kincardine & Deeside	Drum Castle, Drumoak
Perth & Kinross	Auchleeks House, Calvine
Roxburgh	West Leas, Bonchester Bridge
Stewartry of Kirkcudbright	Crossmichael Gardens

Thursday 19 July

Caithness & Sutherland	Castle & Gardens of Mey, Caithness

Saturday 21 July

Fife	Crail: Small Gardens in the Burgh

Sunday 22 July

Aberdeen	Leith Hall, Kennethmont
Ayrshire	Carnell, Hurlford
Clydesdale	Coulter Mains Gardens, Nr. Biggar
Clydesdale	Dippoolbank Cottage, Carnwath
Edinburgh & West Lothian	Lymphoy House, Currie
Fife	Crail: Small Gardens in the Burgh
Kincardine & Deeside	Douneside House, Tarland
Moray & Nairn	Knocknagore, Knockando
Ross, Cromarty, Skye & Inverness	House of Aigas and Field Centre, by Beauly
Roxburgh	Yetholm Village Gardens
Stewartry of Kirkcudbright	The Mill House, Gelston
Stewartry of Kirkcudbright	Millhouse, Rhonehouse
Stirling	14 Glebe Crescent, Tillicoultry
Tweeddale	West Linton Village Gardens
Wigtown	Woodfall Gardens, Glasserton

Saturday 28 July

Caithness & Sutherland	House of Tongue, Tongue, Lairg

Sunday 29 July

Aberdeen	Castle Fraser, Kemnay
Argyll	Ardchattan Priory fete, North Connel
Dumfries	Hallguards Riverside, Hoddam
Fife	Craigfoodie, Dairsie
Moray & Nairn	Bents Green, 10 Pilmuir Rd W., Forres
Perth & Kinross	Hollytree Lodge, Pool O'Muckart

Stewartry of Kirkcudbright .... Arndarroch, St John's Town of Dalry
Stirling .... The Tors, Falkirk
Tweeddale .... Portmore, Eddleston

Saturday 4 August
Edinburgh & West Lothian .... Dr Neil's Garden, Duddingston Vill.

Sunday 5 August
Ayrshire .... Skeldon, Dalrymple
Caithness & Sutherland .... Langwell, Berriedale
Dumfries .... Enterkin Cottage, Dalswinton
Edinburgh & West Lothian .... Dr Neil's Garden, Duddingston Vill.
Kincardine & Deeside .... Glenbervie House, Drumlithie
Midlothian .... Silverburn Village
Perth & Kinross .... Drummond Castle Gardens, Crieff
Stewartry of Kirkcudbright .... Square Point, Crossmichael
Stewartry of Kirkcudbright .... Waterside, Crossmichael
Stirling .... Burnbrae, Killearn
Angus .... Raesmill, Inverkeilor
Caithness & Sutherland .... Langwell, Berriedale

Thursday 9 August
Aberdeen .... The David Welch Winter Gardens

Sunday 12 August
Angus .... Raesmill, Inverkeilor
East Lothian .... The Community Gardens of
                                                           Cockenzie & Port Seton
Caithness & Sutherland .... Langwell, Borriedale
Edinburgh & West Lothian .... South Queensferry Gardens
Isle of Arran .... Brodick Castle & Country Park
Perth & Kinross .... Comrie Village Gardens, Comrie
Perth & Kinross .... Mount Tabor House, Perth
Stewartry of Kirkcudbright .... Cally Gardens, Gatehouse of Fleet

Saturday 18 August
Caithness & Sutherland .... Castle & Gardens of Mey, Caithness

Sunday 19 August
Fife .... Ladies Lake, The Scores, St Andrews
Glasgow & District .... Hill of Birches, Thornton Hall
Renfrew & Inverclyde .... Barshaw Park-Walled Garden, Paisley
Stirling .... Thorntree, Arnprior

Sunday 26 August

Aberdeen .... Pitmedden Gardens, Ellon

Aberdeen .... Tillypronie, Tarland

Fife .... Parleyhill Garden & Manse Garden
                                                                                      Culross

Sunday 2 September

Edinburgh & West Lothian .... 61 Fountainhall Road, Edinburgh

Thursday 6 September

Ross, Cromarty, Skye & Inverness .... Dundonnell House, Wester Ross

Saturday 8 September

Stewarty of Kirkcudbright .... Arndarroch, St John's Town of Dalry

Sunday 9 September

Edinburgh & West Lothian .... 61 Fountainhall Road, Edinburgh

Fife .... Ceres Village Gardens, Cupar

Moray & Nairn .... Gordonstoun, Duffus, Nr. Elgin

Ross, Cromarty, Skye & Inverness .... Inverewe, Poolewe

Stewartry of Kirkcudbright .... Arndarroch, St John's Town of Dalry

Sunday 16 September

Fife .... Cambo House, Kingsbarns

Sunday 23 September

Fife .... Falkland Palace Garden, Falkland

Sunday 7 October

Edinburgh & East Lothian .... 61 Fountainhall Road, Edinburgh

Sunday 21 October

Tweeddale .... Stobo Water Garden, Stobo, Peebles

PLANT SALES 2007
See District Lists for further details

<u>Renfrew & Inverclyde</u>
Carruth, Bridge of Weir
Sunday 3 June 2 - 5pm

<u>Glasgow & District</u>
Glasgow Botanic Gardens
Saturday 9 June 11am - 4pm

<u>Fife</u>
Freuchie Plant Sale
Sunday 16 June Noon - 4pm

<u>Dunbartonshire West</u>
Hill House, Helensburgh
Sunday 2 September 11am - 4pm

<u>Renfrew & Inverclyde</u>
Finlaystone, Langbank
Sunday 2 September 11.30am - 4pm

<u>Fife</u>
Hill of Tarvit, Cupar
Sunday 7 October 10.30 - 4pm

<u>East & Midlothian</u>
Oxenfoord Mains, Dalkeith
Saturday 13 October 9.30 am- 3.30pm

Enjoy Scotland's Gardens in Winter - we've rolled out the white carpet for you!

For further information go to **www.visitscotland.com/snowdrops** or call **0845 119 2811** to listen to the dedicated Snowdrop line detailing what's on in your area week by week.

Live it. Visit Scotland.
visitscotland.com **0845 22 55 121**
The No.1 booking and information service for Scotland.

The Gardens

VisitScotland has teamed up with Scotland's Gardens Scheme, National Trust for Scotland and gardens around the country to bring you the first ever Scottish Snowdrop Festival.

So between 1st February and 11th March 2007, find time to head outdoors and marvel at these angelic little gems in the clarity of light that Winter brings to Scotland. In the crisp air, a woodland walk or a stroll in the gardens of some of Scotland's magnificent castles and historic houses, can blow away the cobwebs and, with the peace and inspiration that the snowdrops infuse, it will work wonders on the soul to boot.

For further information go to **www.visitscotland.com/snowdrops** or call **0845 119 2811** to listen to the dedicated Snowdrop line detailing what's on in your area week by week.

Snowdrop images supplied by Dawyck Botanic Garden.

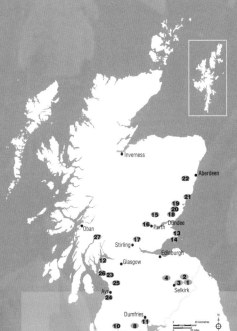

1. FLOORS CASTLE
Kelso, Scottish Borders
t: 01573 223333
w: www.floorscastle.com

2. MELLERSTAIN GARDEN
Gordon, Berwickshire
t: 01573 410225
w: www.mellerstain.com

3. MERTOUN GARDENS
St Boswells, Scottish Borders
t: 01835 823236

4. TRAQUAIR HOUSE
Innerleithen, Peeblesshire
t: 01896 830323
w: www.traquair.co.uk

5. BROUGHTON HOUSE GARDEN
Broughton House,
Kirkcudbright
t: 01557 330437
w: www.nts.org.uk

6. CASTLE KENNEDY
Stair Estates, Rephad,
Stranraer
t: 01776 702024
w: www.castlekennedygardens.co.uk

7. CLACHAN COTTAGE
Gatehouse of Fleet,
Castle Douglas
t: 01557 814444

8. DANEVALE PARK
Crossmichael,
Castle Douglas
t: 01556 670223

9. DUNSKEY GARDENS
Portpatrick, Wigtownshire
t: 01776 810905
w: www.dunskey.com

10. KIRKDALE ESTATE
Carsluith, Newton Stewart,
Wigtownshire
t: 01557 840229

11. UNIVERSITY OF GLASGOW
Crichton Campus,
Dumfries and Galloway
Extra-Mural Group
t: 01557 814215

12. ARDGOWAN GARDEN
Inverkip, Renfrewshire
t: 01475 521656
w: www.ardgowan.co.uk

13. CAMBO GARDENS
Kingsbarns, St Andrews
t: 01333 450054
w: www.camboestate.com

14. KELLIE CASTLE GARDEN
Pittenweem, Fife
t: 01333 720271
w: www.nts.org.uk

15. DIRNANEAN GARDENS
Enochdhu, Near Blairgowrie,
Perthshire
t: 01250 881400

16. FINGASK CASTLE
Rait, Perth
t: 01821 670777
w: www.fingaskcastle.com

17. THE LINNS
Sheriffmuir, Dunblane,
Perthshire
t: 01786 822295

18. GAGIE HOUSE
Duntrune, Dundee
t: 01382 380207
w: www.gagie.com

19. KINNAIRD CASTLE
Brechin, Angus
t: 01674 810209
w: www.southesk.co.uk

20. PITMUIES GARDENS and GROUNDS
Guthrie, by Forfar
t: 01241 828245
w: www.pitmuies.com

21. ECCLESGREIG CASTLE
St Cyrus, Montrose,
Aberdeen & Grampian
t: 01674 850900
w: www.ecclesgreig.com

22. CRATHES CASTLE
Crathes, Banchory,
Aberdeen & Grampian
t: 01330 844744
w: www.nts.org.uk

23. BLAIR ESTATE
Dalry, Ayrshire
t: 01294 833100
w: www.blairestate.com

24. BLAIRQUHAN GARDEN
Blairquhan, Maybole, Ayrshire
t: 01655 770239
w: www.blairquhan.co.uk

25. CAPRINGTON CASTLE
Kilmarnock, Ayrshire
t: 07748 280036

26. KELBURN CASTLE
Fairlie, Ayrshire
t: 01475 568685
w: www.kelburncountrycentre.com

27. ARDKINGLAS
Ardkinglas Estate,
Cairndow, Argyll
t: 01499 600261
w: www.ardkinglas.com

SCOTTISH **SNOWDROP** FESTIVAL

GENERAL INFORMATION

Maps. The maps show the *approximate* locations of gardens. directions can be found in the garden descriptions or full maps on the website at *www.gardensofscotland.org*

Houses are not open unless specifically stated; where the house or part of the house is shown, an additional charge is usually made.

Lavatories. Private gardens do not normally have outside lavatories. For security reasons, owners have been advised not to admit visitors into their houses.

Professional Photographers. No photographs taken in a garden may be used for sale or reproduction without the prior permission of the garden owner.

NEW Garden opening this year for the first time or reopening after a break of six years or more.

♿ Wheelchair access to at least the main features of the garden.

🐕 Dogs on a lead welcomed. **PLEASE NOTE WHERE NO DOG SYMBOL IS SHOWN DOGS, EXCEPT GUIDE DOGS, ARE NOT ALLOWED.**

NCCPG Garden that hold a NCCPG National Plant Collection

❀ Plant stall

☕ Teas normally available at a charge. When there are cream or special teas this is stated in brackets beside the symbol.

❀ Participating in the Scottish Snowdrop Festival. For more details see the Snowdrop Festival Advertisement on pages 28 -29.

The National Trust for Scotland. Members please note that where a National Trust property has allocated an opening day to Scotland's Gardens Scheme which is one of its own normal opening days, members can gain entry on production of their Trust membership card, although donations to Scotland's Gardens Scheme will be most welcome.

Children. All children must be accompanied by an adult.

ABERDEEN

District Organiser   **To be advised**

Area Organisers: **Mrs F G Lawson,** Asloun, Alford AB33 8NR
Mrs A Robertson, Drumblade House, Huntly AB54 6ER
Mrs F M K Tuck, Allargue House, Corgarff AB36 8YP

Treasurer: **Mr J Ludlow**. St Nicholas House, Banchory AB31 5YT

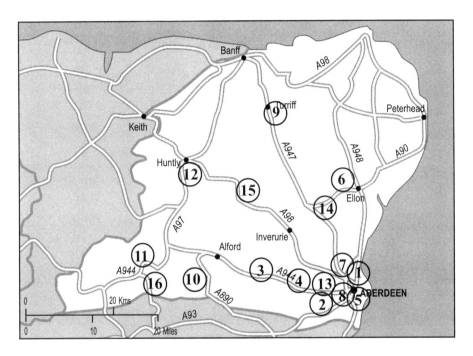

DATES OF OPENING

23 Don Street, Old Aberdeen .... July by appointment Tel 01224 487269
Blairwood, Aberdeen .... Mid June to beginning Oct. by appt.
Tel 01224 86830
Grandhome, Aberdeen .... By appointment Tel 01224 722202
Greenridge, Cults .... July & Aug. by appt. Tel 01224 860200
Hatton Castle, Turriff .... By appointment Tel 01888 562279
Howemill, Craigievar .... By appointment Tel 01975 581278
Kildrummy Castle Gardens, Alford .... Apr - Oct daily Tel 01975 57127/571203
Lochan House, Blackchambers .... Groups by appt. Tel 01224 791753
Ploughman's Hall, Old Rayne .... By appointment Tel 01464 851253

Dunecht House Gardens, Dunecht	Sunday 3 June	1 - 5pm
Kildrummy Castle Gardens, Alford	Sunday 3 June	10am - 5pm
Esslemont, Ellon	Sunday 10 June	1 - 4.30pm
Tillypronie, Tarland	Sunday 10 June	2 - 5pm
Howemill, Craigievar	Sunday 24 June	1.30 - 5pm
Ploughmans Hall, Old Rayne	Sunday 1 July	1 - 6pm
23 Don Street, Old Aberdeen	Sunday 8 July	1.30 - 6pm
Leith Hall, Kennethmont	Sunday 22 July	Noon - 4pm
Castle Fraser, Kemnay	Sunday 29 July	1 - 5pm
The David Welch Winter Gardens, Duthie Park	Thursday 9 August	7pm
Pitmedden Garden, Ellon	Sunday 26 August	1 - 5pm
Tillypronie, Tarland	Sunday 26 August	2 - 5pm

1. 23 DON STREET, Old Aberdeen AB2 1UH

(Miss M & Mr G Mackechnie)

Atmospheric walled garden in historic Old Aberdeen. Wide range of rare and unusual plants and old-fashioned scented roses.

<u>Route:</u> park at St Machar Cathedral, short walk down Chanonry to Don Street, turn right. City plan ref: P7.

<u>Admission</u> £2.50 Concessions £2.00

SUNDAY 8 JULY 1.30 - 6pm

July by appointment Tel: 01224 487269

40% to Cat Protection 60% net to SGS Charities

2. BLAIRWOOD HOUSE, South Deeside Road, Blairs

(Ilse Elders)

Approximately a half acre country garden. Most of it started from scratch seven years ago and still evolving. The garden has been self-designed to provide colour over a long season, without requiring daily care from the owner. Herbaceous borders, small beautiful herb garden packed with well over a hundred medicinal and culinary herbs, pebble mosaics and sunken patio area. One garden 'room' has been grown on a land fill site.

<u>Route:</u> Blairs, on the B9077, 5 mins by car from Bridge of Dee, Aberdeen. Very close to Blairs Museum

<u>Admission</u> £2.50

MID JUNE to BEGINNING OF OCTOBER BY APPOINTMENT Tel: 01224 868301

40% to The Elvanfoot Trust 60% net to SGS Charities

☕ (available at MacDonald Ardoe House Hotel or The Old Mill Inn)

3. CASTLE FRASER, Kemnay AB51 7LD
(The National Trust for Scotland)
Castle Fraser, one of the most spectacular of the Castles of Mar, built between 1575
and 1635 with designed landscape and parkland the work of Thomas White in 1794.
Includes exciting new garden developments. A traditional walled garden of cut
flowers, trees, shrubs and new herbaceous borders. Also a medicinal and culinary
border, organically grown fruit and vegetables. A newly constructed woodland
garden with adventure playground.
Route: near Kemnay, off A944.
Admission £2.50 NTS members £1.50 and Children £1.00
SUNDAY 29 JULY 1 - 5pm
40% to The Gardens Fund of The National Trust for Scotland 60% net to SGS Charities
For other opening details see NTS advert at the back of the book

 (and produce sales) (home baked) Adventure playground

4. DUNECHT HOUSE GARDENS, Dunecht AB3 7AX
(The Hon. Charles A Pearson)
A magnificent copper beech avenue leads to Dunecht House built by John and
William Smith with a Romanesque addition in 1877 by G Edmund Street. Highlights
include rhododendrons, azaleas and a wild garden.
Route: Dunecht 1 mile, routes: A944 and B977.
Admission £3.00 Concessions £1.50
SUNDAY 3 JUNE 1 - 5pm
40% to Riding for the Disabled 60% net to SGS Charities

(partly)

5. THE DAVID WELCH WINTER GARDENS, Aberdeen AB11 7TH
(Aberdeen City Council)
Guided tour on Thursday 9th August with the head gardener. The David Welsh
Winter Gardens consist of over one hectacre of glasshouses and is one of the most
visited in Scotland. They contain a wide range of plant material. Throughout the
temperate house, corridors of perfumes, fern house, Victorian garden, Japanese
garden and tropical house along with one of the largest collection of cacti and
succulents in Britain.
Route: Meet at main entrance.
Admission £4.00
THURSDAY 9 AUGUST 7pm
All takings to Scotland's Gardens Scheme Charities

6. ESSLEMONT, Ellon AB41 8PA
(Mr & Mrs Wolrige Gordon of Esslemont)
Victorian house set in wooded policies above River Ythan. Roses and shrubs in
garden with double yew hedges (17th and 18th centuries).
Route: A920 from Ellon. On Pitmedden/Oldmeldrum road.
Admission: £3.00 Children (4–11 years) and Concessions £2.00
SUNDAY 10 JUNE 1 - 4.30pm
40% to Girl Guiding, Ellon 60% net to SGS Charities

(home baked) Music, Stalls, Charity stalls, Tombola

7. GRANDHOME, Aberdeen AB22 8AR
(Mr & Mrs D R Paton)
18th century walled garden, incorporating rose garden; policies with rhododendrons, azaleas, mature trees and shrubs.
Route: from north end of North Anderson Drive, continue on A90 over Persley Bridge, turning left at Tesco roundabout.
Admission £2.50
BY APPOINTMENT Tel: 01224 722202
40% to Children First   60% net to SGS Charities

  (by arrangement) (at certain times also sometimes fruit and vegetables)

8. GREENRIDGE, Craigton Road, Cults AB51 9PS
(BP Exploration)
Large secluded garden surrounding 1840 Archibald Simpson house, for many years winner of Britain in Bloom 'Best Hidden Garden'. Mature specimen trees and shrubs. Sloping walled rose garden and terraces. Kitchen garden.
Route: directions with booking.
Admission £3.50
JULY & AUGUST BY APPOINTMENT. Tel: 01224 860200 Fax: 01224 860210
40% to Association of the Friends of Raeden   60% net to SGS Charities

 (included in admission price)

9. HATTON CASTLE, Turriff AB54 8ED
(Mr & Mrs James Duff)
Two acre walled garden featuring mixed borders and shrub roses with yew and box hedges and   allees of pleached hornbeam. Kitchen garden and fan trained fruit trees. Lake and woodland walks.
Route: on A947 2 miles south of Turriff.
Admission £4.50 Children free
BY APPOINTMENT Tel: 01888 562279 or E-mail: jjdgardens@btinternet.com
40% to Future Hope 60% net to SGS Charities

♿ (with help) ☕ (and lunch parties, by appointment)

10. HOWEMILL, Craigievar AB33 8TD
(Mr D Atkinson)
Maturing garden with a wide range of unusual alpines, shrubs and herbaceous plants.
Route: from Alford take A980 Alford/Lumphanan road.
Admission £2.50 Children under 12 free
SUNDAY 24 JUNE 1.30 - 5pm
Also by appointment Tel: 01975 581278
40% to Cancer Relief Macmillan Fund 60% net to SGS Charities

♿ (with help) ❀ ☕

11. KILDRUMMY CASTLE GARDENS, Alford AB33 8RA
(Kildrummy Garden Trust)

April shows the gold of the lysichitons in the water garden, and the small bulbs naturalised beside the copy of the 14th century Brig o' Balgownie. Rhododendrons and azaleas from April (frost permitting). September/October brings colchicums and brilliant colour with acers, fothergillas and viburnums.

Route: on A97, 10 miles from Alford, 17 miles from Huntly. Car park free inside hotel main entrance. Coaches park up at hotel delivery entrance.

Admission £3.50 Senior Citizens £3.00 Children free

SUNDAY 3 JUNE 10am - 5pm

April - October daily Tel. 01975 571277/571203. Parties by arrangement.

&(with help) Play area

40% to Aberdeen Branch - Multiple Sclerosis Society 60% net to SGS Charities

www.kildrummy-castle-gardens.co.uk

---

12. LEITH HALL, Kennethmont AB54 4NQ
(The National Trust for Scotland)

This attractive old country house, the earliest part of which dates from 1650, was the home of the Leith and Leith-Hay families for more than three centuries. The west garden was made by Mr and The Hon. Mrs Charles Leith-Hay around the beginning of the twentieth century. The property was given to the Trust in 1945. The rock garden has been enhanced by the Scottish Rock Garden Club in celebration of their 150th anniversary.

Route: on B9002 near Kennethmont.

Admission Garden: £2.50 Concs & Children £1.90

House: £7.00 Concs & Children £5.25

SUNDAY 22 JULY Noon - 4pm

40% to The Gardens Fund of The National Trust for Scotland 60% net to SGS Charities

& (cream) Live music in the garden, Guided walks, Toilet for disabled visitors.

---

13. LOCHAN HOUSE, Blackchambers, nr Blackburn AB32 7BU
(Mrs M Jones)

Evolving country garden of 1½ acres. Includes ponds, and waterfowl collection, Herbaceous plantings, formal courtyard and ornamental grass garden. Recently planted wildlife shelterbelt with paths and fine views to Bennachie.

Route: A96, 2 miles south of Kinellar roundabout, follow signs for Millbuie.

Admission £3.00 Accompanied children free.

GROUPS BY APPOINTMENT TEL: 01224 791753

40% to Breast Cancer Research, Aberdeen 60% net to SGS Charities

& (with help)

14. PITMEDDEN GARDEN, Ellon AB41 0PD
(The National Trust for Scotland)

Garden created by Lord Pitmedden in 1675. Elaborate floral designs in parterres of box edging, inspired by the garden at the Palace of Holyroodhouse, have been re-created by the Trust. Fountains and sundials make fine centrepieces to the garden, filled in summer with 40,000 annual flowers. Also herb garden, herbaceous borders and trained fruit, plant sales, Museum of Farming Life, Visitor Centre, nature hut, woodland walk and wildlife garden.

Admission £5.00 Concessions & children £4.00   Special rates for pre-booked coach parties.

SUNDAY 26 AUGUST 1 - 5pm

40% to The Gardens Fund of The National Trust for Scotland 60% net to SGS Charities

   Museum of farming life and visitor centre

---

15. PLOUGHMAN'S HALL, Old Rayne AB52 6SD
(Mr & Mrs A Gardner)

One acre garden. Rock, herbaceous, kitchen, herb and woodland gardens.

Route: off A96, 9 miles north of Inverurie.

Admission £2.00 Children 50p

SUNDAY 1 JULY 1 - 6pm

Also by appointment Tel. 01464 851253

40% to Wycliffe Bible Translators 60% net to SGS Charities

 (with help)   Craft stalls

---

16. TILLYPRONIE, Tarland AB34 4XX
(The Hon Philip Astor)

Late Victorian house for which Queen Victoria laid foundation stone. Herbaceous borders, terraced garden, heather beds, water garden and new rockery. New Golden Jubilee garden still being laid out. Shrubs and ornamental trees, including pinetum with rare specimens. Fruit garden and greenhouses. Superb views. In June there is a wonderful show of azaleas and spring heathers.

Route: between Ballater and Strathdon, off A97.

Admission £3.00 Children £1.50

SUNDAY 10 JUNE 2 - 5pm

SUNDAY 26 AUGUST 2 - 5pm

All proceeds to Scotland's Gardens Scheme

 (only June opening)  (cream)

ANGUS

District Organiser:	**Mrs Nici Rymer,** Nether Finlarg, Forfar DD8 1XQ
Area Organisers:	**Mrs T Dobson,** Logie House, Kirriemuir DD8
	Miss Ruth Dundas, Caddam, Kinnordy, Kirriemuir DD8 4LP
	Mrs J Henderson, Mains of Panmuir, by Carnoustie DD7
	Mrs R Porter, West Scryne, By Carnoustie DD7 6LL
	Mrs C Smoor, Gagie House, Tealing, Dundee DD4 0PR
	Mrs G Stewart, Ugiebank, Edzell DD9
	Mrs A Stormonth Darling, Lednathie, Glen Prosen, Kirriemuir DD8
Treasurer:	**Col R H B Learoyd,** Wedderburn, 9b The Glebe, Edzell DD9 7SZ

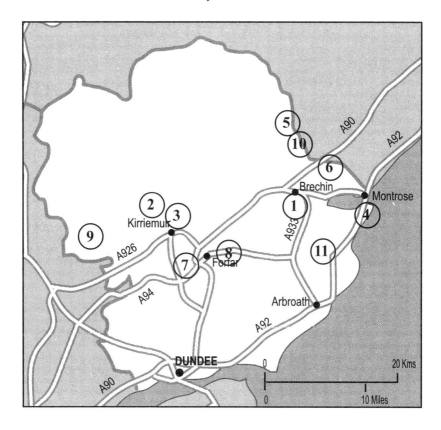

DATES OF OPENING

House of Pitmuies, Guthrie .... 1 April - 31 October   10am - 5pm
Melgam House, Lintrathen, Kirriemuir .... 1 April - 30 September   9am - dusk

37

Brechin Castle, Brechin	Sunday 13 May	2 - 5.30pm
Dalfruin, Kirriemuir	Sunday 20 May	2 - 5pm
Dunninald, Montrose	Sunday 20 May	2 - 5pm
Cortachy Castle, Kirriemuir	Sunday 3 June	2 - 6pm
Newtonmill House, by Edzell	Sunday 24 June	2 - 5.30pm
Edzell Village, ...	Sunday 1 July	2 - 5pm
Gallery, Montrose	Sunday 8 July	2 - 5pm
Glamis Castle, Glamis	Sunday 15 July	10am - 6pm
Raesmill, Inverkeilor	Sunday 12 August	2 - 5pm

1. BRECHIN CASTLE, Brechin DD9 6SH
(The Earl & Countess of Dalhousie)
Ancient fortress of Scottish kings on cliff overlooking River Southesk. Rebuilt by
Alexander Edward – completed in 1711. Extensive walled garden 300 yards from
Castle with ancient and new plantings and mown lawn approach. Rhododendrons,
azaleas, bulbs, interesting trees, wild garden.
Route: A90, Brechin 1 mile.
Admission £3.50 OAP's £2.50 Children under 12 free
SUNDAY 13 MAY 2 - 5.30pm
20% to Dalhousie Day Centre 20% to Unicorn Preservation Society 60% net to SGS Charities
 (in garden)

2. CORTACHY CASTLE, Kirriemuir DD8 4LY
(The Earl & Countess of Airlie)
16th century castellated house. Additions in 1872 by David Bryce. Spring garden and
wild pond garden with azaleas, primroses and rhododendrons. Garden of fine
American species trees and river walk along South Esk.
Route: B955 Kirriemuir 5 miles.
Admission £3.50
SUNDAY 3 JUNE 2 - 6pm
40% to McManus Galleries, Dundee 60% net to SGS Charities
  Plant raffle, Children's quiz

3. DALFRUIN, Kirktonhill Road, Kirriemuir DD8 4HU
(Mr & Mrs James A Welsh)
A well-stocked mature garden of almost one-third of an acre situated at end of cul-
de-sac. Unusual plants, dactylorhiza, tree peonies, meconopsis, trilliums. Stream
added in Autumn 2000 (Newts first seen autumn 2003!).
Route: from centre of Kirriemuir turn left up Roods; Kirktonhill Road is on left near
top of hill, just before the school 20mph zone. Please park on Roods or at St Mary's
Church.
Admission £2.50 Accompanied children free
SUNDAY 20 MAY 2 - 5pm
*20% to The Glens & Kirriemuir Old Parish Church 20% St Mary's Scottish Episcopal Church
60% net to SGS Charities*
♿ (with assistance- grass paths just wide enough)   ☕ (at St Mary's Church)

4. DUNNINALD, Montrose DD10 9TD
(The Stansfeld Family)
Traditional walled garden with mixed borders, vegetables, fruit trees, greenhouse. Extensive grounds with drifts of bluebells and beech avenue. Castle built in 1823 by James Gillespie Graham.
Route: 2 miles south of Montrose off A92 off Lunan/Montrose road.
Admission £2.50 Children under 12 free
SUNDAY 20 MAY 2 - 5pm
40% to The British Red Cross 60% net to SGS Charities

---

5. EDZELL VILLAGE, Edzell DD9 7TT
Walk round 10 gardens in Edzell village. Tickets are on sale in the village and a plan is issued with the tickets.
Admission £2.50 Children 50p
SUNDAY 1 JULY 2 - 5pm
40% to Stracathro Cancer Care Fund UK 60% net to SGS Charities

---

6. GALLERY, Montrose DD10 9LA
(Mr & Mrs John Simson)
Redesign and replanting of this historic garden have preserved and extended its traditional framework of holly, privet and box. A grassed central alley, embellished with circles, links interesting theme gardens and lawns. A short walk leads to the raised bank of the North River Esk with views towards the Howe of the Mearns. From that point rough paths lead west and east along the bank.
Route: From A90 immediately south of Northwater Bridge take exit to 'Hillside' and next left to 'Gallery & Marykirk'. Or from A937 immediately west of rail underpass follow signs to 'Gallery & Northwater Bridge'.
Admission £2.50 Children 50p
SUNDAY 8 JULY 2 - 5pm
40% to Practical Action 60% net to SGS Charities

---

7. GLAMIS CASTLE, Glamis DD8 1RJ
(The Earl & Countess of Strathmore & Kinghorne)
Family home of the Earls of Strathmore and a royal residence since 1372. Childhood home of HM Queen Elizabeth The Queen Mother, birthplace of HRH The Princess Margaret, and legendary setting for Shakespeare's play 'Macbeth'. Five-storey L-shaped tower block dating from 15th century, remodelled 1600, containing magnificent rooms with wide range of historic pictures, furniture, porcelain etc. Spacious grounds with river and woodland walks through pinetum and nature trail. Walled garden exhibition. Formal garden.
For this day only the greenhouses and famous vine collection will be open.
Route: Glamis 1 mile A94.
Admission: Grounds only £3.70 Children & OAPs £2.70
　　　　　Castle & grounds: £7.50 OAPs £6.30 Children £4.30
SUNDAY 15 JULY 10am - 6pm
40% to Princess Royal Trust for Carers 60% net to SGS Charities

 (restaurant) Shopping pavilion

---

8. HOUSE OF PITMUIES, Guthrie, By Forfar

(Mrs Farquhar Ogilvie)

Two semi-formal wall gardens adjoin 18th century house and shelter long borders of herbaceous perennials, superb delphiniums, old fashioned roses and pavings with violas and dianthus. Spacious lawns, river and lochside walks beneath fine trees. A wide variety of shrubs with good autumn colours. Massed spring bulbs, interesting turreted doocot and "Gothick" wash-house.

Route A932. Friockheim 1½ miles.

Admission £2.50

1 APRIL - 31 OCTOBER 10am - 5pm

Donations to Scotland's Gardens Scheme

 (rare and unusual), Fruit in season

---

9. MELGAM HOUSE, Lintrathen DD8 5JH **NEW**

(Michael & Carolyn Anstice)

A mid 18th century restored manse garden of approximately 2½ acres beside Lintrathen Loch. The grounds include a terraced walled garden that descends to the river Melgam. Elsewhere are climbing roses, herbaceous borders and shrubs. There are also some impressive trees. The garden includes a riverside walk and a magnificent waterfall that can be viewed from above or visited by the more agile. There are also many bulbs in the spring. Small vegetable garden.

Route: B951 from Kirriemuir to Glenilsa, turn left to Lintrathen and first left to church. B954 from Alyth and 2 miles from Peel Farm

Admission £2.50

1 APRIL - 30 SEPTEMBER 9am - dusk

40% to St Mary's Kirriemuir 60% net to SGS Charities

---

10. NEWTONMILL HOUSE, by Edzell DD9 7PZ

(Mr & Mrs Stephen Rickman)

A walled garden comprising herbaceous borders, rose and peony beds, vegetable beds and doocot. Formal layout with view to house.

Route: B966 Brechin/Edzell road

Admission £2.50 Children free

SUNDAY 24 JUNE 2 – 5.30pm

40% to Riding for the Disabled 60% net to SGS Charities

---

11. RAESMILL, Inverkeilor DD11 5SN **NEW**

(Ann Hay)

The garden surrounds Raesmill House. At the back of house was an old mill pond which leaked water over the years and had been out of bounds. Now this area has been transformed into a sheltered garden but still has a natural/wild feel about it.

Route: From Inverkeilor go out Station Road, follow road for 1 mile, take right turning (signposted Ethie, Auchmithrie, Arbroath), then take left turn (Ethie), Raesmill is the second white farmhouse on left.

Admission £3.00 OAP's £2.00 Children free

SUNDAY 12 AUGUST 2 - 5pm

40% to The Cystic Fibrosis Trust 60% net to SGS Charities

ARGYLL

District Organiser
& Treasurer:

Mrs Minette Struthers, Ardmaddy Castle, Balvicar by
Oban PA34 4QY

Area Organisers:

Mrs Gill Cadzow, Duachy, Kilninver, Oban PA34 4RH
Mrs Elizabeth Ingleby, Braighbhaille, Crarae, Inveraray
PA32 8YA
Mrs Catherine Shaw, Kilbrandon House, Balvicar, by Oban,
Argyll PA34 4RA
Mrs Mary Thomson, Glenbranter House, By Strachur, Argyll
PA27 8DJ

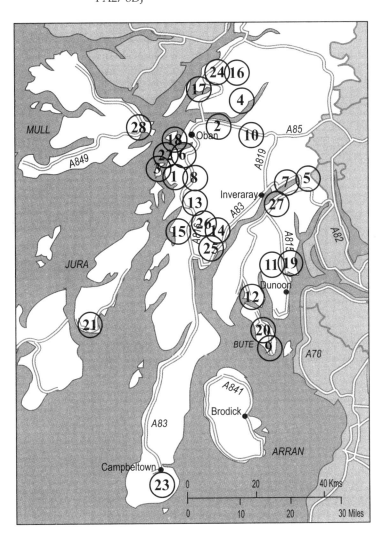

DATES OF OPENING

Achnacloich, Connel...	8 April - 31 October daily	10am - 6pm
An Cala, Ellenabeich	1 April - 31 October daily	10am - 6pm
Ardchattan Priory, North Connel	1 April - 31 October daily	9am - 6pm
Ardkinglas Woodland Garden.	All year daily	daylight hours
Ardmaddy Castle, by Oban	All year daily	9am - sunset
	or by appointment	Tel. 01852 300353
Ardno, Cairndow	By appointment	Tel. 01499 302304
Ascog Hall, Isle of Bute	Wed - Sun Easter - End Oct.	10am - 5pm
Barguillean's "Angus Garden"	All year daily	9am - 6pm
Cnoc-na-Garrie, Ballymeanoch	By appointment	Tel. 01546 605327
Druimavuic House, Appin	April, May & June daily	10am - 6pm
Druimneil House, Port Appin.	1 April - 31 October daily	9am - 6pm
Eckford, By Dunoon	9 April - 6 June daily	10am - 5pm
Glecknabae, Isle of Bute	Spring - Autumn by appointment	
		Tel. 01700 505655
Jura House, Ardfin, Isle of Jura	Open all year	9am - 5pm
Kildalloig, Campbeltown.	By appointment	Tel. 01586 553192
Kinlochlaich House Gardens, Appin	Open all year 9.30am -5.30pm (or dusk)	
(Except Sundays Oct. - March)	Sundays April - Sept. 10.30am - 5.30pm	
Torosay Castle Gardens, Isle of Mull	Open all year	

Benmore Botanic Garden, Dunoon	Sunday 22 April	10am - 6pm
Arduaine, Kilmelford	Sat & Sun 5 & 6 May	9.30am - 6pm
Knock Cottage, Lochgair	Sat & Sun 12 & 13 May	2 - 5pm
Crinan Hotel Garden, Crinan	Sunday 13 May	11am - 5pm
Minard Castle, Minard	Sunday 13 May	2 - 6pm
Colintraive Gardens, ...	Sat & Sun 19 & 20 May	1 - 5pm
Kilbrandon, Balvicar	Sat & Sun 19 & 20 May	1 - 5pm
Knock Cottage, Lochgair	Sat & Sun 19 & 20 May	2 - 5pm
Duachy, Kilninver	Sunday 20 May	1 - 5pm
Strachur House Flower & Woodland Gardens	Sat & Sun 26 & 27 May	1- 5pm
Crarae Garden, Inveraray	Sat & Sun 9 & 10 June	9.30am - 6pm
Achnacille, Kilmelford, By Oban	Sat & Sun 16 & 17 June	2 - 6pm
Glecknabae, Rothesay	Sunday 24 June	1 - 4.30pm
Ardchattan Priory Fete, Connel	Sunday 29 July	Noon - 4pm

1. ACHNACILLE, Kilmelford by Oban PA34 4XD

Mr & Mrs Robin Asbury)

Created from a hillside a few years ago, a one acre garden at the head of Loch Melfort with sweeping views down the Loch. Varied plantings of trees, shrubs and herbaceous. Pond and streamside plants and a small rock garden.

Route: ½ mile from Kilmelford (A816) on road signposted 'Degnish'

Admission £2.50 Children free

SATURDAY & SUNDAY 16 & 17 JUNE 2 - 6pm

40% to Scripture Union Scotland 60% net to SGS Charities

Scotland's Gardens Scheme

Gardens open for charity

PERTH & KINROSS GARDENS OPEN IN 2008

Gardens Open By Arrangement

Cluniemore, Pitlochry	1 May - 1 October	Tel: 01796 472006
Easter Meikle Fardle, Meikleour	1 April - 30 Sept. 10am - 6.30pm	Tel: 01738 710330
Rossie House, Forgandenny	1 March - 31 October	Tel: 01738 812265
Wester Dalqueich, Carnbo	1 June - 31 August 2pm - dusk	Tel: 01577 840229

Gardens Open Regularly

Ardvorlich, Lochearnhead	3rd May - 1st June	9am - dusk
Bolfracks, Aberfeldy	1 April - 31 October	10am - 6pm
Braco Castle, Braco	1 February - 31 October	10am - 5pm
Cluny House, Aberfeldy	March to 31 October	10am - 6pm
Dowhill, Kelty	May - Tuesdays & Thursdays	10am - 4pm
Glendoick, by Perth	18 February - 14 March	10am - 4pm
Glendoick, by Perth	May - Saturdays & Sundays	2pm - 5pm
Glendoick, by Perth	7 April - 6 June Mondays-Fridays	10am - 4pm
Scone Palace, Perth	16 - 17 & 22 - 24 February	11am - 4pm
Scone Palace, Perth	21 March - 31 October	9.30am - 5.45pm (Sat 5pm)
Scone Palace, Perth	1 November - 29 February (Fridays)	10am - 4pm

Gardens Open On a Specific Date

Megginch Castle, Errol	Sunday 06 April	2pm - 5pm
Glendoick, by Perth	Sunday 04 May	2pm - 5pm
Branklyn, Perth	Sunday 11 May	10am - 5pm
Glendoick, by Perth	Sunday 18 May	2pm - 5pm
Meikleour House, by Blairgowrie	Sunday 18 May	2pm - 5pm
Cloan, by Auchterarder	Sunday 25 May	1.30pm - 5.30pm
Gleneagles, By Auchterarder	Sunday 01 June	2pm - 5pm
Balnakeilly, Pitlochry	Sunday 08 June	2pm - 5.30pm
House of Aldie, Fossoway, Kinross	Sunday 08 June	2pm - 5.30pm
Comrie Village Gardens, Comrie	Sunday 15 June	1pm - 5pm
Explorers Garden, Pitlochry	Sunday 15 June	10am - 5pm
Bradystone House, Murthly	Sunday 22 June	11am - 4pm
Blair Castle Gardens, Blair Atholl	**Thursday** 26 June	9.30am - 5.30pm
Carig Dhubh, Bonskeid	Sunday 29 June	11am - 5pm
The Cottage, Longforgan	Sunday 29 June	2pm - 5pm
Wester Cloquhat, Bridge of Cally	Sunday 06 July	2pm - 5pm
Auchleeks House, Calvine	Sunday 13 July	2pm - 5.30pm
Glenlyon House, Fortingall	Sunday 20 July	2pm - 5pm
Boreland, Killin	Sunday 27 July	2pm - 5.30pm
Drummond Castle Gardens, Crieff	Sunday 03 August	1pm - 5pm
Cluniemore, Pitlochry	Sunday 10 August	2pm - 5pm
Comrie Village Gardens, Comrie	Sunday 17 August	1pm - 5pm
Machany, Auchterarder	Sunday 07 September	11am - 4pm
Battleby, Redgorton	Sunday 05 October	1pm - 4pm

www.gardensofscotland.org

Charity No: SC011337

Scotland's Gardens Scheme

Gardens open for charity

PERTH & KINROSS GARDENS OPEN IN 2008

Gardens Open By Arrangement

Cluniemore, Pitlochry	1 May - 1 October	Tel: 01796 472006
Easter Meikle Fardle, Meikleour	1 April - 30 Sept. 10am - 6.30pm	Tel: 01738 710330
Rossie House, Forgandenny	1 March - 31 October	Tel: 01738 812265
Wester Dalqueich, Carnbo	1 June - 31 August 2pm - dusk	Tel: 01577 840229

Gardens Open Regularly

Ardvorlich, Lochearnhead	3rd May - 1st June	9am - dusk
Bolfracks, Aberfeldy	1 April - 31 October	10am - 6pm
Braco Castle, Braco	1 February - 31 October	10am - 5pm
Cluny House, Aberfeldy	March to 31 October	10am - 6pm
Dowhill, Kelty	May - Tuesdays & Thursdays	10am - 4pm
Glendoick, by Perth	18 February - 14 March	10am - 4pm
Glendoick, by Perth	May - Saturdays & Sundays	2pm - 5pm
Glendoick, by Perth	7 April - 6 June Mondays-Fridays	10am - 4pm
Scone Palace, Perth	16 - 17 & 22 - 24 February	11am - 4pm
Scone Palace, Perth	21 March - 31 October	9.30am - 5.45pm (Sat 5pm)
Scone Palace, Perth	1 November - 29 February (Fridays)	10am - 4pm

Gardens Open On a Specific Date

Megginch Castle, Errol	Sunday 06 April	2pm - 5pm
Glendoick, by Perth	Sunday 04 May	2pm - 5pm
Branklyn, Perth	Sunday 11 May	10am - 5pm
Glendoick, by Perth	Sunday 18 May	2pm - 5pm
Meikleour House, by Blairgowrie	Sunday 18 May	2pm - 5pm
Cloan, by Auchterarder	Sunday 25 May	1.30pm - 5.30pm
Gleneagles, By Auchterarder	Sunday 01 June	2pm - 5pm
Balnakeilly, Pitlochry	Sunday 08 June	2pm - 5.30pm
House of Aldie, Fossoway, Kinross	Sunday 08 June	2pm - 5.30pm
Comrie Village Gardens, Comrie	Sunday 15 June	1pm - 5pm
Explorers Garden, Pitlochry	Sunday 15 June	10am - 5pm
Bradystone House, Murthly	Sunday 22 June	11am - 4pm
Blair Castle Gardens, Blair Atholl	**Thursday** 26 June	9.30am - 5.30pm
Carig Dhubh, Bonskeid	Sunday 29 June	11am - 5pm
The Cottage, Longforgan	Sunday 29 June	2pm - 5pm
Wester Cloquhat, Bridge of Cally	Sunday 06 July	2pm - 5pm
Auchleeks House, Calvine	Sunday 13 July	2pm - 5.30pm
Glenlyon House, Fortingall	Sunday 20 July	2pm - 5pm
Boreland, Killin	Sunday 27 July	2pm - 5.30pm
Drummond Castle Gardens, Crieff	Sunday 03 August	1pm - 5pm
Cluniemore, Pitlochry	Sunday 10 August	2pm - 5pm
Comrie Village Gardens, Comrie	Sunday 17 August	1pm - 5pm
Machany, Auchterarder	Sunday 07 September	11am - 4pm
Battleby, Redgorton	Sunday 05 October	1pm - 4pm

www.gardensofscotland.org

Charity No: SC011337

2. ACHNACLOICH, Connel PA37 1OR

(Mrs T E Nelson)
Scottish baronial house by John Starforth of Glasgow. Succession of bulbs, flowering shrubs, rhododendrons, azaleas, magnolias and primulas. Woodland garden with ponds above Loch Etive. Good Autumn colours.
Route: on the A85 3 miles east of Connel.
Admission £3.00   Children free OAPs £1.00
8 APRIL - 31 OCTOBER DAILY 10am - 6pm
All takings to Scotland's Gardens Scheme

3. AN CALA, Ellenabeich, Isle of Seil PA34 4QY

(Mrs Thomas Downie)
A small garden of under five acres designed in the 1930s, An Cala sits snugly in its horse-shoe shelter of surrounding cliffs. A very pretty garden with streams, waterfall, ponds, many herbaceous plants as well as azaleas, rhododendrons and cherry trees in spring.
Route: proceed south from Oban on Campbeltown road for 8 miles, turn right at Easdale sign, a further 8 miles on B844; garden between school and village.
Admission £2.50 Children free
1 APRIL - 31 OCTOBER DAILY 10am - 6pm
Donation to Scotland's Gardens Scheme

4. ARDCHATTAN PRIORY, North Connel PA37 1RQ

(Mrs Sarah Troughton)
Beautifully situated on the north side of Loch Etive. The Priory, founded in 1230, is now a private house. The ruins of the chapel and graveyard, with fine early stones, are in the care of Historic Scotland and open with the garden. The front of the house has a rockery, extensive herbaceous and rose borders, with excellent views over Loch Etive. To the west of the house there are shrub borders and a wild garden, numerous roses and over 30 different varieties of sorbus providing excellent autumn colour.
Route: Oban 10 miles. From north, turn left off A828 at Barcaldine on to B845 for 6 miles. From Oban or the east on A85, cross Connel Bridge and turn first right, proceed east on Bonawe Road. Well signed.
Admission £2.50 Children free
1 APRIL - 31 OCTOBER DAILY 9am - 6pm
A fete will be held on SUNDAY 29 JULY Noon - 4pm
Donation to Scotland's Gardens Scheme

5. ARDKINGLAS WOODLAND GARDEN, Cairndow PA26 8BH
(Ardkinglas Estate)
In peaceful setting overlooking Loch Fyne the garden contains one of the finest collections of rhododendrons and conifers in Britain. This includes the mightiest conifer in Europe and one of Britain's tallest trees as well as many other champion trees. Gazebo with unique "Scriptorium" based around a collection of literary quotes. Woodland lochan, ancient mill ruins and many woodland walks. Scottish Tourist Board 3* Garden.
Route: entrance through Cairndow village off A83 Loch Lomond/Inveraray road.
Admission £3.50 Children under 16 years free.
ALL YEAR ROUND, DAYLIGHT HOURS
Donation to Scotland's Gardens Scheme

 Gift sales Picnic facilities Toilets

---

6. ARDMADDY CASTLE, Balvicar, by Oban PA34 4QY
(Mr & Mrs Charles Struthers)
Ardmaddy Castle, with its woodlands and formal walled garden on one side and spectacular views to the islands and the sea on the other, has many fine rhododendrons and azaleas with a variety of trees, shrubs, unusual vegetables and flower borders between dwarf box hedges. Daffodils and bluebell woods. Recently created water gardens and stoneworks add increasing interest to this continuously developing garden.
Route: Oban 13 miles, Easdale 3 miles. 1½ miles of narrow road off B844 to Easdale.
Admission £2.50 Children 50p
ALL YEAR DAILY 9am - sunset
Also visits by arrangement: Tel. 01852 300353
Donations to Scotland's Gardens Scheme

♿ (mostly) (and veg./fruit when available) Toilet suitable for disabled.

---

7. ARDNO, Cairndow PA26 8BE
(Kate How)
Begun in 1992 - an overgrown canvas in need of extensive clearing. 12 years on it is becoming well established with interesting trees and shrubs around the house, through the beautiful wooded gorge and down to the Loch via the meadow/ arboretum. The site is stunning and the garden is maturing amazingly quickly. Interesting for those planning to start from scratch!
Route: situated at the top end of Loch Fyne betweeen Cairndow and St Catherines, off the A815.
Admission £2.50 Children free
BY APPOINTMENT Tel: 01499 302304 - Michael & Karen Bowyer
40% to S J Noble Trust 60% net to SGS Charities

8. ARDUAINE, Kilmelford PA34 4XQ

(The National Trust for Scotland)

An outstanding 20 acre coastal garden on the Sound of Jura. Begun more than 100 years ago on the south facing slope of a promontory separating Asknish Bay from Loch Melfort, this remarkable hidden paradise, protected by tall shelterbelts and influenced favourably by the Gulf Stream, grows a wide variety of plants from the four corners of the globe. Internationally known for the rhododendron species collection, the garden also features magnolias, camellias, azaleas and many other wonderful trees and shrubs, many of which are tender and not often seen. A broad selection of perennials, bulbs, ferns and water plants ensure a year-long season of interest.

Route: off the A816 Oban - Lochgilphead, sharing an entrance with the Loch Melfort Hotel.

Admission Adults £5.00 Concessions £4.00 Under 5s free Family £14.00

SATURDAY & SUNDAY 5 & 6 MAY 9.30am - 6pm

40% to The Gardens Fund of The National Trust for Scotland   60% net to SGS Charities

---

9. ASCOG HALL, Ascog, Isle of Bute PA20 9EU

(Mr & Mrs W Fyfe)

Recently restored after decades of neglect, this appealing garden is continuing to develop and mature, with an abundance of choice plants and shrubs which delight the eye from spring to autumn. It includes a formal rose garden with a profusion of fragrant old shrub roses. Through a rustic ivy-clad stone arch which in bygone years led to the tennis court, there is now a large gravel garden with sun-loving plants and grasses. Undoubtedly, however, the most outstanding feature is our acclaimed Victorian fernery. This rare and beautiful structure houses subtropical and temperate fern species, including an ancient Todea barbara - the only survivor from the original collection, and said to be around 1,000 years old.

Admission £3.00 Children free, under supervision.

DAILY (Except Mons & Tues) EASTER - END OCTOBER 10am - 5pm

Donation to Scotland's Gardens Scheme

---

10. BARGUILLEAN'S "ANGUS GARDEN", Taynuilt PA35 1HY

(Mr Robin Marshall)

Nine acre woodland garden around an eleven acre loch set in the Glen Lonan hills. Spring flowering shrubs and bulbs, extensive collection of rhododendron hybrids, deciduous azaleas, conifers and unusual trees. The garden contains a large collection of North American rhododendron hybrids from famous comtemporary plant breeders. Some paths can be steep. 3 marked walks from 30 minutes to $1\frac{1}{2}$ hours.

Route: 3 miles south off A85 Glasgow/Oban road at Taynuilt; road marked Glen Lonan; 3 miles up single track road; turn right at sign.

Admission £2.00 Children free

DAILY ALL YEAR 9am - 6pm

Coach tours by arrangement. Contact Sean Honeyman Tel 01866 822 335

Donation to Scotland's Gardens Scheme

11. BENMORE BOTANIC GARDEN, Dunoon PA23 8QU

(Regional Garden of the Royal Botanic Garden Edinburgh and one of the National Botanic Gardens of Scotland)

World famous for its magnificent conifers and its extensive range of flowering trees and shrubs, including over 250 species of rhododendron. From a spectacular avenue of Giant Redwoods, numerous waymarked walks lead the visitor via a formal garden and pond through hillside woodlands to a dramatic viewpoint overlooking the Eachaig valley and the Holy Loch.

Route: 7 miles north of Dunoon or 22 miles south from Glen Kinglass below Rest and Be Thankful pass; on A815.

Admission £3.50 Concessions £3.00 Children £1.00 Families £8.00

SUNDAY 22 APRIL 10am - 6pm

Donation to Scotland's Gardens Scheme

For further details see advert at back of book

&. (limited due to hill slopes) James Duncan Cafe (licensed), Botanics Shop for gifts and plants, Courtyard Gallery with events and exhibitions

12. COLINTRAIVE GARDENS PA21 2EB

Four spring and woodland gardens in this very beautiful corner of Argyll. They are of varied interest and within easy reach of each other on the old B866 shore road looking out over Loch Riddon and the Kyles of Bute.

The Community Garden is beside the village hall, just past the ferry terminal. This garden was created by the community for the 'Beechgrove Garden' programme in 2003 and is now reaching maturity. A viewing platform over the Milton Burn and waterfall was added in 2005.

1. **Breamanach**   (Anne Neal)
2. **Caol Ruadh**   (Karen and Colin Scotland)
3. **Colintraive Community Gardens** NEW (Sara Maclean)
4. **Dunyvaig**   (Moyra Donald)

Route: off A866 (Dunoon 20 miles via B836, Strachur 22 miles)

Admission £3.00 includes all 4 gardens Children free.

Tickets and maps obtainable at all gardens.

SATURDAY & SUNDAY 19 & 20 MAY 1 - 5pm

All takings to Scotland's Gardens Scheme

 (in village hall) Exhibition of work by local artists in village hall

13. CNOC-NA-GARRIE, Ballymeanoch, by Lochgilphead PA31 8QE

(Mrs Dorothy Thomson)

A garden being created from rough hillside, designed for year-round interest. Large range of alpines, shrubs, grasses, herbaceous plants and bulbs, many grown from seed.

Route: 2 miles south of Kilmartin, A816. Entrance sharp left between cottages and red brick house, continue up track to bungalow.

Admission £2.50 Accompanied children free.

BY APPOINTMENT TEL. 01546 605327

20% to British Red Cross Society (mid Argyll) 20% to Cancer Relief Macmillan Fund
60% net to SGS Charities

14. CRARAE GARDEN, Inveraray PA32 8YA

(The National Trust for Scotland)

A spectacular 50 acre garden in a dramatic setting. Crarae has a wonderful collection of woody plants centered on the Crarae Burn, which is spanned by several bridges and tumbles through a rocky gorge in a series of cascades. A wide variety of shrubs and trees, chosen for spring flowering and autumn colour grow in the shelter of towering conifers and the lush, naturalistic planting and rushing water gives the garden the feel of a valley in the Himalayas. Sturdy shoes advised.

Route: 11 miles south of Inverarary/12 miles north of Lochgilphead on A83.

Admission £5.00 Concessions £4.00 Under 5s free Family £14.00 (Correct at time of going to press)

SATURDAY & SUNDAY 9 & 10 JUNE 9.30am - 6pm

Donation to Scotland's Gardens Scheme

 (only Lower Gardens)

15. CRINAN HOTEL GARDEN, Crinan PA31 8SR

(Mr & Mrs N Ryan)

Small rock garden with azaleas and rhododendrons created into a steep hillside over a century ago with steps leading to a sheltered, secluded garden with sloping lawns, herbaceous beds and spectacular views of the canal and Crinan Loch.

Route: Lochgilphead A83, then A816 to Oban, then A841 Cairnbaan to Crinan.

Admission £2.00 Accompanied children free

SUNDAY 13 MAY 11am - 5pm

40% to Feedback Madagascar   60% net to SGS Charities

 (at coffee shop beside canal basin)   Raffle - a painting of flowers by Frances Macdonald

16. DRUIMAVUIC HOUSE, Appin PA38 4BQ

(Mr & Mrs Newman Burberry)

Stream, wall and woodland gardens with lovely views over Loch Creran. Spring bulbs, rhododendrons, azaleas, primulas, meconopsis, violas.

Route: A828 Oban/Fort William, 4 miles south of Appin. At end of new bridge bear left at roundabout. At the north end road is signed Invercreran, at the south end road is signed "Local Traffic". Two miles from either end, look for private road where public signs warn of flooding.

Admission £2.50 Children free

APRIL, MAY & JUNE DAILY 10am - 6pm

30% to Alzheimer Scotland - Action on Dementia (Oban & Lorne Branch)   70% net to SGS Charities

  (interesting)

17. DRUIMNEIL HOUSE, Port Appin PA38 4DQ

(Mrs J Glaisher) (Gardener - Mr Andrew Ritchie)

Ten acre garden overlooking Loch Linnhe with many fine varieties of mature trees and rhododendrons and other woodland shrubs.

Route: turn in Appin off A828 (Connel/Fort William road). 2 miles, sharp left at Airds Hotel, second house on right.

Admission Donations

1 APRIL - 31 OCTOBER DAILY 9am - 6pm

All takings to Scotland's Gardens Scheme

 (home baking)   Lunches by prior arrangement - Tel: 01631 730228

18. DUACHY, Kilninver PA34 4QU **NEW**

(Gill Cadzow)

³/₄ acre garden with extensive collection of rhododendrons and azaleas. Three ponds with a variety of primulas. Part of the garden is on a slope - need sturdy shoes.

Route: 8 miles south of Oban (B816) turn right onto B844 after 3 miles you come to a loch on the left hand side, on the right is a white house with lawns going down to the road (Duachy).

Admission £2.50   School children free   £4.00 joint with Kilbrandon

SUNDAY 20 MAY 1 - 5pm

40% Argyll Animal Aid 60% net to SGS Charities

  (home baking)

19. ECKFORD, By Dunoon PA23 8QU

(Mr D Younger)

For many years closely connected with the Benmore Botanic Garden, Eckford has a 4 acre woodland garden of immense charm sited on a hillside. The general public will enjoy the massed blooms of rhododendrons and azaleas, and the specialist gardener will notice unusual specimens of trees and shrubs that have been planted over the past 100 years. This is a wild garden, so sturdy shoes are advised.

Route: Eckford lies just off the A815 about 6¹/₂ miles north of Dunoon and ¹/₂ mile south of Benmore Garden.

Admission £2.50

9 APRIL - 6 JUNE DAILY 10am - 5pm

40% John Younger Trust   60% net to SGS Charities

 (when available)

20. GLECKNABAE, Rothesay PA20 0QX
(Iain & Margaret Gimblett)
A south-facing hillside garden in the least known part of the island of Bute with
magnificent views to the mountains of Arran. A collection of formal courtyard
gardens, all different, with rock, boulder and bog gardens as well as shrubs and trees.
This unusual garden is welcoming and inspirational.
Route: A844 to Ettrick Bay, signposted off the coast road between Rhubodach and
Rothesay; continue to end of 'made up' road; approximately 5 miles.
Admission Tickets for 24 June: £5.00 Children under 16 free
SUNDAY 24 JUNE 1 - 4.30pm (a 'Music in the Garden' day)
Bring own picnic to celebrate Mid Summer; undercover if wet.
Spring - Autumn by appointment Tel: 01700 505655 E-mail: gimblettsmill@aol.com
Admission By Donation
Individuals or small parties welcome
20% The Raven Trust 20% RNLI   60% net to SGS Charities

 (partially)

---

21. JURA HOUSE, Ardfin, Isle of Jura HG3 5QY
(The Ardfin Trust)
Organic walled garden with wide variety of unusual plants and shrubs, including large
Australasian collection. Also interesting woodland and cliff walk, spectacular views.
Points of historical interest, abundant wild life and flowers.
Route: 5 miles east from ferry terminal on A846. Ferries to Islay from Kennacraig by
Tarbert.
Admission £2.50 Children under 16 £1.00
ALL YEAR 9am - 5pm
Donation to Scotland's Gardens Scheme

 (June, July and August)   Toilet

---

22. KILBRANDON, Balvicar PA34 4RA NEW
(The Hon. Michael Shaw)
The designed landscape, affording a pleasant seaside outlook for a regency house,
was largely the work of Lord and Lady Kilbrandon between 1951 and 1991. The
associated garden and woodlands feature numerous rhododendrons and azaleas,
with a variety of other trees and shrubs running almost to the water's edge. The
regency walled garden is almost entirely decorative preserving the orignal
herbaceous borders and capitalising on a largely frost-free environment. There are
some interesting specimens and the overall effect is much enhanced by a
remarkable natural setting.
Route: take A816 south from Oban, 8 miles. Turn right on B844 (signed Easdale) 7
miles. At Balvicar take B8003 (signed Cuan) 1 mile Entrance on left at Kilbrandon
Church.
Admission £2.50 School children free £4.00 joint ticket with Duachy on Sunday 20 May
SATURDAY & SUNDAY 19 & 20 MAY 1 - 5pm
40% to Save the Children (North Argyll) 60% net to SGS Charities

23. KILDALLOIG, Campbeltown PA28 6RE

(Mr & Mrs Joe Turner)

Coastal garden with some interesting and unusual shrubs and herbaceous perennials. Woodland walk. Pond area under construction.

<u>Route:</u> A83 to Campbeltown, then 3 miles south east of town past Davaar Island.

<u>Admission</u> £2.00 Accompanied children free.

BY APPOINTMENT. Tel: 01586 553192.

40% to Royal National Lifeboat Institution 60% net to Scotland's Gardens Scheme

 (partially)

---

24. KINLOCHLAICH HOUSE GARDENS, Appin PA38 4BD

(Mr & Mrs D E Hutchison & Miss F M M Hutchison)

Walled garden, incorporating the West Highlands' largest Nursery Garden Centre. Garden with beds of alpines, heathers, primulas, shrubs, rhododendrons, azaleas and herbaceous plants. Fruiting and flowering shrubs and trees. Woodland walk. Spring garden.

<u>Route:</u> A828. Oban 18 miles, Fort William 27 miles. Bus stops at gate by Police Station.

<u>Admission</u> Donations

ALL YEAR 9.30am - 5.30pm or dusk <u>except</u> Sundays October - March

APRIL - SEPTEMBER SUNDAYS 10.30am - 5.30pm

Closed Christmas & New Year, except by appointment

40% to Appin Village Hall 60% net to SGS Charities

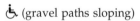 (gravel paths sloping)

---

25. KNOCK COTTAGE, Lochgair PA31 8RZ **NEW**

(Mr & Mrs David Sillar)

A five acre woodland and water garden centred round a small loch and a lily pond. Shrubs and trees were planted around the house in the late 1960's but the present garden began with the creation of the 'lochan' in 1989 and the plantings of the 1990's; development continues. Camelias, rhododendrons, azaleas and other shrub species are sheltered by mixed conifers eucalyptus, birch, rowan, alder and beech. Several of the 50 different rhododendrons are scented including Rh. 'fragrantissimum' and some early flowering varieties. The garden is quite level but access is by grassed paths so waterproof footwear is recomended.

<u>Route:</u> Half mile south of Lochgair Hotel on A83, on the west side of the road between two sharp bends.

<u>Admission</u> £3.00

SATURDAY & SUNDAY 12 & 13 MAY 2-5pm

SATURDAY & SUNDAY 19 & 20 MAY 2 - 5pm

40% to Save the Children 60% net to SGS Charities

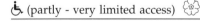 (partly - very limited access)

26. MINARD CASTLE, Minard PA32 8YB [NEW]
(Mr & Mrs Reinold Gayre)
Though much of the 75 acres (30 hectares) surrounding Minard Castle is planted with Christmas trees, the parkland has many fine mature specimens of unusual conifers and deciduous trees. Of particular note are the two weeping ash trees in front of the house and behind the building, a loderi 'King George' rhododendron with wonderfully scented flowers and a large Crinodendron hookerianum with waxy red pendant flowers. Paths meander among the trees and the multitude of different rhododendrons, at their most beautiful in April and May, some of them planted recently as eventual replacements for those dating from the 19th century. To the west of the house a walled garden has formally arranged paths, flower beds and several greenhouses. North of this is a large pond beyond which many interesting rhododendrons from the Himalayas and elsewhere are becoming established.
<u>Admission</u> £3.00 Children free
SUNDAY 13 MAY 2 - 6pm
40% to 60% net to Scotland's Gardens Scheme

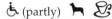 (partly)

27. STRACHUR HOUSE FLOWER & WOODLAND GARDENS PA27 8BX
(Sir Charles & Lady Maclean)
Directly behind Strachur House, the flower garden is sheltered by magnificent beeches, limes, ancient yews and Japanese maples. There are herbaceous borders, a burnside rhododendron and azalea walk and a rockery. Old fashioned and species roses, lilies, tulips, spring bulbs and Himalayan poppies make a varied display in this informal haven of beauty and tranquillity. The garden gives onto Strachur Park, laid out by General Campbell in 1782, which offers spectacular walks through natural woodlands with 200-year-old trees, rare shrubs and a lochan rich in native wildlife.
<u>Route:</u> turn off A815 at Strachur House Farm entrance; park in farm square.
<u>Admission</u> £2.50 Children 50p
SATURDAY & SUNDAY 26 & 27 MAY 1 - 5pm   FLOWER GARDEN
40% to CLASP 60% net to SGS Charities

28. TOROSAY CASTLE & GARDENS, Isle of Mull PA65 6AY
(Mr Christopher James)
Torosay is a beautiful and welcoming family home completed in 1858 by David Bryce in the Scottish Baronial style and is surrounded by 12 acres of spectacular contrasting gardens which include formal terraces and an impressive Italian statue walk, surrounded by informal woodland and water gardens. Many rare and tender plants.
<u>Route:</u> 1¹/₂ miles from Craignure, A849 south. N.G. rail steam/diesel from Craignure. Regular daily ferry service from Oban to Craignure.
<u>Admission to Castle & Gardens</u> £5.50 Children £3.00 Concessions £5.00
with reduced admission when Castle closed
GARDENS OPEN ALL YEAR
CASTLE OPEN 1 APRIL - 31 OCTOBER 10.30am - 5.00pm
Groups welcome
Donation to Scotland's Gardens Scheme

 (Tearoom) Gift shop Adventure playground

AYRSHIRE

Joint District Organisers: **Mrs R F Cuninghame,** Caprington Castle, Kilmarnock KA2 9AA
Mrs John Greenall, Lagg House, Dunure KA7 4LE

Area Organisers: **Mrs Michael Findlay,** Carnell, Hurlford, Kilmarnock KA1 5JS
Mrs R Lewis, St. John's Cottage, Maybole KA19 7LN
Mrs John Mackay, Pierhill, Annbank, Ayr KA6 5AW
Miss Catriona Hepburn, Ladyburn, By Maybole KA19 7SG

Treasurer: **Mr Hywel Davies,** Peatland, Gatehead, Kilmarnock KA2 9AN

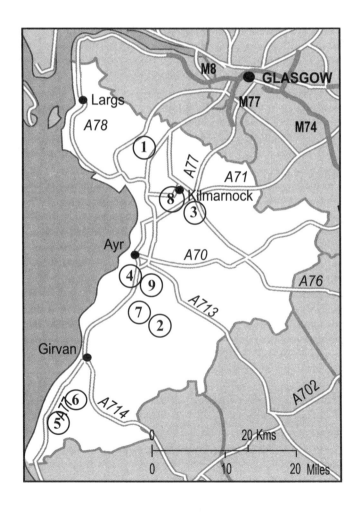

DATES OF OPENING

Blairquhan, Straiton	Sunday 25 Febuary	12 - 4pm
Kirkhill Castle, Colmonell	Sunday 20 May	2 - 5pm
Doonholm, Ayr	Sunday 27 May	2 - 5pm
Blair House, Dalry	Sunday 17 June	2 - 5.30pm
Ladyburn, By Maybole.	Sunday 24 June	2 - 5pm
Penkill Castle, near Girvan	Sunday 1 July	2 - 5pm
Knockdolian, Colmonell	Sunday 15 July	2 - 5pm
Carnell, Hurleford	Sunday 22 July	2 - 5pm
Skeldon, Dalrymple	Sunday 5 August	2 - 5pm

1. BLAIR HOUSE, Dalry KA24 4ER

(Mr & Mrs Luke Borwick)

The extensive and fine-timbered policies surrounding this tower house of great antiquity, are first mentioned by Pont in the early 17th century. The well laid out park is attributed to Captain William Fordyce Blair RN in the 1850s. Visitors are permitted to walk through these delightful historic grounds all the year round. Particularly spectacular are the spring and early summer gardens, with continuous interest from the drifts of snowdrops and bluebells, to the species rhododendrons and azaleas. Recent renovations to the Private gardens are providing year round interest. For Scotland's Gardens Scheme the private gardens at Blair House and the Carriage House will be open.

Route: Enter by North Lodge. From A737 in Dalry, follow signs to Railway Station. Drive through the Housing Estate, just after the farm on right hand side you will see the entrance at North Lodge.

Admission £3.50 Children £2.50 Families £10.00 Concessions £2.50

SUNDAY 17 JUNE 2-5.30pm

40% to Friedreicks Ataxia   60% net to SGS Charities.

♿ (partly) ✿ ☕ Face painting

2. BLAIRQUHAN, Straiton, Maybole KA19 7LZ

(Sir Patrick & Lady Hunter Blair)

Regency Castle built by William Burn, 1821 - 1842 for Sir David Hunter Blair 3rd Bart. Sixty-foot high saloon with gallery. The kitchen courtyard is formed with stones and sculpture from an earlier castle. 3 mile private drive along the River Girvan. Walled garden, pinetum and Regency glasshouse. The Castle is surrounded by an extensive park including an arboretum. There is a tree trail and a shop.

Route: Near Kirkmichael, follow AA signs. Entry from B7045 over bridge half mile south of Kirkmichael.

Admission £6.00 Children £3.00 Concessions £4.00 (including tour of house)

SUNDAY 25 FEBUARY 12 - 4pm SNOWDROP AND TREE TRAIL

40% to Ayrshire Rivers Trust   60% net to SGS Charities

♿ ☕ (in house)

3. CARNELL, Hurlford KA1 5JS
(Mr & Mrs J R Findlay & Mr & Mrs Michael Findlay)
Alterations in 1843 by William Burn. 16th century Peel Tower. 5 acres of gardens and landscaped grounds and 100 metre phlox and shrub border. Extensive and spectacular herbaceous borders around Carnell House.
Route: from A77 (Glasgow/Kilmarnock) take A76 (Mauchline/Dumfries) then right on to the A719 to Ayr for 1½ miles.
Admission £3.00 School children free.
SUNDAY 22 JULY 2 - 5pm
40% between Craigie Parish Church & Craigie Village Hall, Marie Curie Cancer Care and British Red Cross Society 60% net to SGS Charities

 (cream) Ice cream, Craft stalls, Silver band,
Special display by the Scottish Delphinium Society

4. DOONHOLM, Ayr KA6 6BL
(Mr and Mrs Peter Kennedy)
Informal gardens in attractive setting on the banks of the River Doon. Mature trees, shrubs and marvellous show of rhododendrons and azaleas.
Route: Signposted from Burns Cottage, Alloway and from A77.
Admission £3.00 School children free
SUNDAY 27 MAY 2 - 5pm
40% between Ayrshire Rivers Trust and Alloway Kirk Bandawe Malawi appeal 60% net to SGS Charities

 (limited)

5. KIRKHILL CASTLE, Colmonell KA26 0SB **NEW**
(Mr and Mrs Paul Gibbons)
8½ acre garden with rhododendrons, magnolias and camellias. Azalea walk, rose garden, glass houses and woodland walkways.
Route: Kirkhill Castle is in Colmonell Village next to the village hall.
Admission £3.50 School children free
SUNDAY 20 MAY 2 - 5pm
40% to Colmonell Primary School 60% net to SGS Charities

 (partly) (home baked)

6. KNOCKDOLIAN, Colmonell KA26 0LB
(Lord and Lady Richard Wellesley)
A beautiful garden set within a spectacular landscape of river and hills. 1¼ acres of walled garden, herbaceous borders, greenhouses and a classical peach case. Extensive rhododendrons and azaleas, all planted within the last 10 years mostly around the house and in the policies and along the river. Remains of fortified house built C1620.
Route: 1½ miles from Colmonell, 3½ miles from Ballantrae on the junction of B734 and B7044.
Admission £3.50 School children free
SUNDAY 15 JULY 2 - 5pm
40% to Ayrshire Rivers Trust 60% net to SGS Charities

 (partly)

7. LADYBURN, By Maybole KA19 7SG
(Mr and Mrs David Hepburn and Miss Catriona Hepburn)
This old garden has been extensively re-designed and re-planted. Features include a burnside walk, herbaceous and shrub borders and a pond with marginal plantings. The garden now holds four national collections of roses whilst four further collections are currently being established.
Route: Off B7023/B741 Maybole/Crosshill/Dailly road signposted to 'Campsite'.
Admission £3.50 Children 50p
SUNDAY 24 JUNE 2 - 5pm
40% to Straiton & Kirkmichael Parish Churches 60% net to SGS Charities

8. PENKILL CASTLE, near Girvan KA26 9TQ
(Mr & Mrs Patrick Dromgoole)
A series of three Victorian gardens, one formal, one landscaped and one originally for vegetables, linked together by a 'wild walk' overlooking a burn leading to the Penwhapple River.
Route: 3 miles east of Girvn on Old Dailly to Barr road B734.
Admission £3.00 School children free
SUNDAY 1 JULY 2 - 5pm
40% to Barr Parish Church 60% net to SGS Charities

 (limited) Stalls. Bagpipes and Scottish dancing

9. SKELDON, Dalrymple KA6 6AT
(Mr S E Brodie QC)
One and a half acres of formal garden with herbaceous borders and arched pathways. Large Victorian glasshouse with a substantial collection of plants. Four acres of woodland garden within a unique setting on the banks of the River Doon.
Route: from Dalrymple take B7034 Dalrymple/Hollybush Road.
Admission £3.00 School children free
SUNDAY 5 AUGUST 2 - 5pm
40% to Princes Royal Trust for Carers 60% net to SGS Charities

 (home baked) Silver band on the lawn.

Our website, www.gardensofscotland.org, provides information on Scotland's Gardens Scheme and the gardens that open for us.

The site will be re-designed in the course of 2007

BERWICKSHIRE

District Organiser:	**Mrs F Wills**, Anton's Hill, Coldstream TD12 4JD
Area Organisers:	**Mrs C Bailey,** Summerhill, Beanburn, Ayton TD14 5QY
	Miss Anthea Montgomery, Crooks Cottage, Hirsel, Coldstream TD12 4LR
Treasurer:	**Col S J Furness,** The Garden House, Netherbyres, Eyemouth TD14 5SE

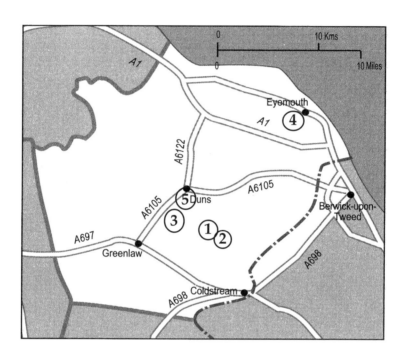

DATES OF OPENING

Bughtrig, Leitholm	1 June - 1 Sept daily	11am-5pm
Netherbyres, Eyemouth	By appt. (for parties 10 or over) Tel. 018907 50337	
Charterhall, Duns	Sunday 20 May	2 - 5.30pm
Whitchester House, Berwickshire	Sunday 3 June	2 - 5.30pm
Antons Hill, Leitholm	Sunday 24 June	2 - 6pm
Netherbryres, Eyemouth	Sunday 8 July	2 - 5.30pm

1. ANTONS HILL, Leitholm TD12 4JD

(Mr & Mrs Wills, Alec West & Pat Watson)
Well treed mature garden which has been improved and added to since 1999. There are woodland walks including a stumpery and large well planted pond, shrubberies and herbaceous borders together with a restored organic walled garden and greenhouse with a pear and apple orchard.
Route: signed off B6461 west of Leitholm.
Admission £3.00 Children under 16 free
SUNDAY 24 JUNE 2 - 6pm
40% to Oakfield (East Maudit) Ltd (Home for people with special needs) 60% net to SGS Charities

 (large) free rides on model railway

2. BUGHTRIG, Near Leitholm, Coldstream TD12 4JP

(Major General & The Hon Mrs Charles Ramsay)
A traditional hedged Scottish family garden with an interesting combination of herbaceous plants, shrubs, annuals and fruit. It is surrounded by fine specimen trees which provide remarkable shelter.
Route: half mile east of Leitholm on B6461.
Admission £2.50 Children under 18 £1.00
1 JUNE TO 1 SEPTEMBER DAILY 11am - 5pm
Donation to Scotland's Gardens Scheme

(mainly) Small picnic area
Special arrangements, to include house visit, possible for bona fide groups.
Accommodation in house possible for 4–8 guests. Contact tel: 01890 840678

3. CHARTERHALL, Duns TD11 3RE

(Major & Mrs A Trotter)
Mature rhododendrons and azaleas in a woodland garden surounding a lovely family home with an outstanding view. Flower garden of roses, bulbs and perennial plants. Walled garden with newly designed vegetable garden and new greenhouse, which includes a small orchid house.
Route: 6 miles south-west of Duns, 3 miles east of Greenlaw, B6460.
Admission Adults £3.00 Children £1.00
SUNDAY 20 MAY 2 - 5.30pm
40% to Prostate Research Cancer Centre 60% net to SGS Charities

 Cake stall , Plant naming competition

4. NETHERBYRES, Eyemouth TD14 5SE

(Col S J Furness & Perennial (GRBS))
A unique 18th century elliptical walled garden. Daffodils and wild flowers in the spring. Annuals, roses, herbaceous borders, fruit and vegetables in the summer.
Route: ½ mile south of Eyemouth on A1107 to Berwick.
Admission £3.00 Concessions £1.50
SUNDAY 8 JULY 2 - 5.30pm
40% to Perennial (GRBS) 60% net to SGS Charities

(in house)
Parties of 10 or more by appointment at any time Tel: 018907 50337

5. WHITCHESTER HOUSE, Duns TD11 3SF
(Teen Challenge)
A once famous rhododendron garden, now being brought back to life by young amateur gardeners, resident in the house. The lost garden of Berwickshire!
Route: B6355 Duns to Gifford road, turn off at Ellenford.
Admission £3.00   Concessions £2.00 Children free
SUNDAY 3 JUNE 2 - 5.30pm
40% to Teen Challenge   60% net to Scotland's Gardens Scheme

♿ (partly)

CAITHNESS & SUTHERLAND

District Organiser: **Mrs Judith Middlemas,** 22 Miller Place, Scrabster, Thurso, Caithness. KW14 7UH

Area Organiser: **Mrs Jonny Shaw,** Amat, Ardgay, Sutherland IV24 3BS

Treasurer: **Captain Colin Farley-Sutton**, RN DL Shepherd's Cottage, Watten, Caithness KW1 5UP

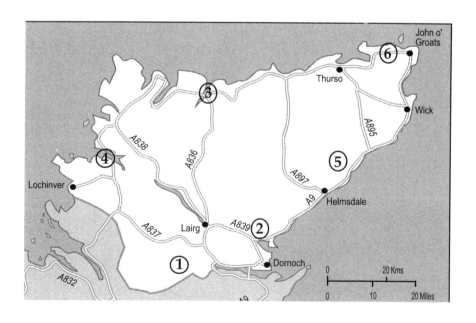

DATES OF OPENING

Kerrachar, Kylesku .... Mid May - mid Sept Tues, Thurs & Suns
and by appointment Tel. 01571 833288
Langwell, Berriedale .... By appointment Tel. 01593 751278

Amat, Ardgay .... Sat & Sun 9 & 10 June   2- 5pm
Dunrobin Castle, Golspie .... Saturday 30 June   10.30am - 5.30pm
The Castle & Gardens of Mey, Caithness .... Wednesday 11 July   10.30am - 4pm
The Castle & Gardens of Mey, Caithness .... Thursday 19 July   10.30am - 4pm
House of Tongue, Tongue .... Saturday 28 July   2 - 6pm
Langwell, Berriedale .... Sunday 5 August   2 - 5pm
Langwell, Berriedale .... Sunday 12 August   2 - 5pm
The Castle & Gardens of Mey, Caithness .... Saturday 18 August   10.30am - 4pm

1. AMAT, Ardgay IV34 3BS
(Jonny and Sara Shaw)
Riverside garden set in Amat forrest. Old and new rhododendrons. Woodland and river walk.
Route: take road from Ardgay to Croick 9 miles.
Admission £3.00 Children 50p
SATURDAY & SUNDAY 9 & 10 JUNE 2 - 5pm
40% between Croick Church & Help The Aged Charities   60% net to SGS Charities
 (partially) ☕

2. DUNROBIN CASTLE & GARDENS, Golspie KW10 6RR
(The Sutherland Trust)
Formal gardens laid out in 1850 by the architect, Barry. Set beneath the fairytale castle of Dunrobin.
Route: castle one mile north of Golspie on A9.
Admission £7.00   OAP's £6.00   Children £5.00   Students £6.00   Family ticket £19.00
Group admission (minimum 10 people) Adults £6.00   OAPs £5.50
SATURDAY 30 JUNE 10.30am - 5.30pm (Last admission 5pm)
40% to Police Dependants Trust 60% net to SGS Charities
♿ (by prior arrangement) ☕ (and gift shop in castle) Picnic site and woodland walks, Dunrobin Castle Museum in gardens, Stunning falconry display

3. HOUSE OF TONGUE, Tongue, Lairg IV27 4YF
(The Countess of Sutherland)
17th century house on Kyle of Tongue. Walled garden, herbaceous borders, old fashioned roses.
Route: Tongue half a mile. House just off main road approaching causeway.
Admission to garden £3.00 OAP'S £2.00 Children 50p
SATURDAY 28 JULY 2 - 6pm
40% to Children 1st 60% net to SGS Charities
♿ (partially) ☕

4. KERRACHAR, Kylesku IV27 4HP
(Peter & Trisha Kohn)
Plantsman's garden and small nursery beautifully located in an extremely remote and wild coastal setting. Wide range of hardy perennials and shrubs. Featured on 'BBC Gardeners' World' in 2006 and selected by 'The Independent' as one of its '10 best gardens to visit in summer'.
Route: access only by 25 minute boat journey from Kylesku (approx £10).
All sailings at 13.00 from Kylesku (Old Ferry Pier)
Garden admission £3.00 Children free
MID MAY TO MID SEPTEMBER TUESDAYS, THURSDAYS AND SUNDAYS
Additional visits for groups by arrangement. Tel: 01571 833288
email: info@kerrachar.co.uk Website: www.kerrachar.co.uk
40% to Myfanwy Townsend Melanoma Research Fund 60% net to SGS Charities

5. LANGWELL, Berriedale KW7 6HD
(The Lady Anne Bentinck)
A beautiful old walled-in garden situated in the secluded Langwell strath. Charming access drive with a chance to see deer.
Route: A9 Berriedale 2 miles.
Admission £3.00 Children under 12 free OAPs £2.50
SUNDAY 5 AUGUST 2 - 5pm
SUNDAY 12 AUGUST 2 - 5pm
Also by appointment. Tel: 01593 751278
40% to RNLI 60% net to SGS Charities

  (served under cover) Cars free

6. THE CASTLE & GARDENS OF MEY, Caithness IV2 6XB
(The Queen Elizabeth Castle of Mey Trust)
Originally a Z plan castle bought by the Queen Mother in 1952 and then restored and improved. The walled garden and the East Garden were also created by the Queen Mother.
Route: on A836 between Thurso and John O'Groats, 1½ miles from Mey.
Admission Gardens only: £3.00 Concession £2.50
                 Castle and Gardens: £7.50 Concessions £6.50 Children £3.00
WEDNESDAY 11 JULY 10.30am - 4.00pm
THURSDAY 19 JULY 10.30am - 4.00pm
SATURDAY 18 AUGUST 10.30am - 4.00pm
40% Queen's Nursing Institute (Scotland) 60% net to SGS Charities

♿ (served in Visitors Centre)

website: www.castleofmey.org.uk

CLYDESDALE

District Organiser: **Mrs M Maxwell Stuart,** Baitlaws, Lamington ML12 6HR

Area Organiser: **Mrs Irene Miller,** West End, 4 Main Street, Carnwath ML11 8JZ
                        PR - Mr G Crouch, 113 High Street, Biggar ML12 6DL

Treasurer: **Mrs Edna Munro,** High Meadows, Nemphlar, Lanark ML11 9JF

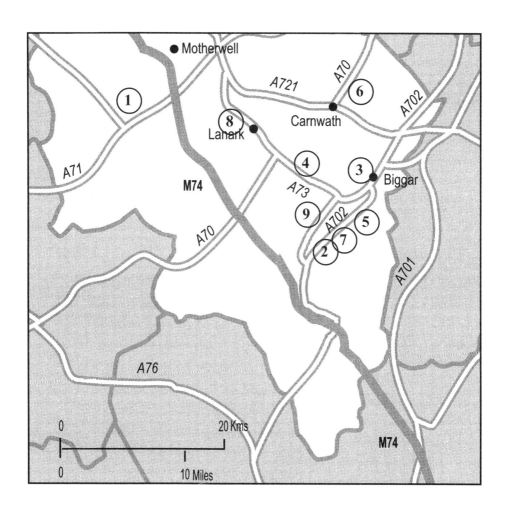

DATES OF OPENING

Baitlaws, Lamington	June, July, Aug. by appt.	01899 850240
Carmichael Mill, Lanark	By appointment	01555 665880

Lamington Village & Overburns	Sunday 10 June	2 - 5pm
Nemphlar Village Garden Trail	Sunday 10 June	1.30 - 5.30pm
Dippoolbank Cottage, Carnwath	Sunday 17 June	2 - 6pm
20 Smithycroft, Hamilton	Sunday 24 June	1 - 5pm
Wyndales Cottage, Symington	Sunday 8 July	12 - 5pm
Biggar Park, Biggar	Sunday 15 July	2 - 6pm
Coulter Mains Gardens, Near Biggar	Sunday 22 July	2 - 6pm
Dippoolbank Cottage, Carnwath	Sunday 22 July	2 - 6pm

1. 20 SMITHYCROFT, Hamilton ML3 7UL
(Mr & Mrs R.I. Fionda)
A plantswoman's garden which has been developed over the past seven years.
Eucalyptus, phormiums and clematis abound and there is a large range of unusual
plants which only flourish in sheltered parts of Scotland.
<u>Route:</u> off M74 at Junction 6. 1mile on A72, well signed.
<u>Admission</u> £3.00 Children free
SUNDAY 24 JUNE 1 - 5pm
40% to Friends of Saint Mary (South African Clinic) 60% net to SGS Charities

---

2. BAITLAWS, Lamington, Biggar ML12 6HR
(Mr & Mrs M Maxwell Stuart)
The garden is set at over 900ft above sea level and has been developed over the past
twenty five years with a particular emphasis on colour combinations of shrubs and
herbaceous perennials which flourish at that height. The surrounding hills make an
imposing backdrop. Featured in 'Good Gardens Guide'
<u>Route:</u> off A702 above Lamington village. Biggar 5 miles, Abington 5 miles, Lanark 10 miles.
<u>Admission</u> £3.50 Children under 12 free
JUNE, JULY & AUGUST BY APPOINTMENT Tel. 01899 850240
40% to Biggar Museum Trust, Lamington Chapel Restoration Fund 60% net to SGS Charities

---

3. BIGGAR PARK, Biggar ML12 6JS
(Mr & Mrs David Barnes)
Ten acre garden starred in 'Good Gardens Guide', featured on 'The Beechgrove
Garden' and in 'Country Life' 'Scottish Field' and many others. Incorporating traditional walled garden with long stretches of herbaceous borders, shrubberies, fruit,
vegetables and a potager. Lawns, walks, pools, Japanese garden and other interesting features. Glades of rhododendrons, azaleas and blue poppies in May and June. Good
collection of old fashioned and new species roses in July. Interesting young trees.
<u>Route:</u> on A702, quarter mile south of Biggar.
<u>Admission</u> £4.00 concessions £3.50 (nice children free)
SUNDAY 15 JULY 2 - 6pm
40% to Chest Heart & Stroke, Scotland 60% net to SGS Charities

 (partially) (home baking)

---

4. CARMICHAEL MILL, Hyndford Bridge, Lanark ML11 8SJ
(Chris, Ken & Gemma Fawell)
Riverside gardens which surround the only remaining workable water powered grain mill on the whole of the River Clyde a few miles upstream from the World Heritage New Lanark Textile Mills. Informal and wild gardens with fruit and vegetables with herbaceous and shrub plantings and riverside walks. Newly created still pond and bog gardens with mass plantings of Primula candelabra and Meconopsis grandis. Also to be seen are the archaeological remains of mediaeval grain mills from c. 1200 and foundry, lint mill and threshing mill activity.
Route: just off A73 Lanark to Biggar Road half a mile east of the Hyndford Bridge.
Admission to gardens and mill £3.50 OAPs & Children over 12 £2.00
BY APPOINTMENT ONLY Tel. 01555 665880
Donation to SGS Charities

♿ (partially) (refreshments by prior booking)

---

5. COULTER MAINS GARDENS, Coulter, nr. Biggar ML12 6PR `NEW`
(Sir Graeme and Lady Davies)
Opening for the first time, are 'new' gardens, developed over the last six years in an established setting. They include various water features, conifer and acer plantations, a maze, a traditional border and a riotous late summer garden. Planting in a new walled garden, featuring N.Z plants began in 2006.
Route: South of Biggar, off 702
Admission £3.50 Children under 12 free
SUNDAY 22 JULY 2 - 6pm
40% between Coulter Library and Biggar Museum Trust 60% net to SGS Charities

 (most gardens are accessible)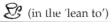

---

6. DIPPOOLBANK COTTAGE, Carnwath ML11 8LP
(Mr Allan Brash)
Artist's intriguing cottage garden. Vegetables grown in small beds. Herbs, fruit, flowers. Garden now extended to include pond, with flowers, trees, etc. Wooden toadstools. Tree house now completed.
Route: off B7016, 2½ miles Carnwath. Well signed.
Admission £3.00 Children free
SUNDAYS 17 JUNE & 22 JULY 2 - 6pm
40% to Cancer Relief Macmillan Fund 60% net to SGS Charities

✿  (in the 'lean to')

7. LAMINGTON VILLAGE AND OVERBURNS, Lamington ML12 **NEW**

Lamington

A beautiful conservation village with a fine view of Tinto. Several village gardens are open, each with its unique character.

Overburns

(Mr & Mrs M Scott)

A newly created garden opening for the first time. It is set along a fast-flowing burn and specialises in rare primulas, meconopsis and irises.

Route: Lamington on the A702 between Biggar (5 miles) Abington (5 miles) and 10 miles from Lanark. Overburns is off the A702 four miles from Biggar.

Admission £3.50 (inclusive)

SUNDAY 10 JUNE 2 - 5pm

40% to Biggar Museum Trust Lamington Chapel Restoration Fund   60% net to SGS Charities

  (in village hall)   Garden trail guide, duck race and stalls

---

8. NEMPHLAR VILLAGE GARDEN TRAIL, Nemphlar, Lanark ML11 9JG

A varied selection of gardens with extensive views over the Clyde Valley. A pleasant stroll of 1 mile covers all gardens.

Route: leave A73 at Cartland Bridge or A72 (Clyde Valley Road) at Crossford.

Admission £3.00 Children under 14 free

SUNDAY 10 JUNE 1.30 - 5.30pm

40% to St Andrew's Hospice, Airdrie   60% net to SGS Charities

  (in village hall)

---

9. WYNDALES COTTAGE, Symington, Biggar ML12 6JU **NEW**

(John & Judy Rutherford)

This is a new garden and therefore not very mature in plants. It is a mixture of woodland, herbaceous and water garden. There are stunning views of the surrounding hills from the garden.

Route: The garden is situated on A73 four miles west of Biggar, approximately halfway between Lanark and Abington. Left hand side going North.

Admission £3.00 Children free

SUNDAY 8 JULY 12 - 5pm

40% to The Gillespie Centre Biggar Refurbishment Fund 60% net to SGS Charities

 (partly)

Celebrations

of

Scotland's Gardens Scheme's

75th Anniversary

Threave 30 May 2006. Joint celebration of Scotland's Gardens Scheme and the National Trust for Scotland's 75th Anniversary.

TRH the Duke and Duchess of Rothesay admiring the rhododendron presented to her, our President, by our former Chairman, Mrs Robin Hunt.

Crieff 13 June 2006 Queens Nursing Institute Scotland annual lunch.
Our former Chairman, Mrs Robin Hunt, being presented with an
anniversary cake by QNIS.

Hill of Tarvit 6 June 2006 Garden Party celebrating our anniversary.
Our former Chairman, Mrs Robin Hunt, cutting the anniversary cake.

Hill of Tarvit 6 June 2006 Garden Party celebrating our anniversary.
Our former Chairman, Mrs Robin Hunt, drawing raffle numbers.

Hill of Tarvit 6 June 2006 Garden Party celebrating our anniversary.
Our former Chairman, Mrs Robin Hunt, addressing our guests.

'Gardening Scotland' 2 -4 June 2006.
A section of the stand and garden we shared with Dobbies Garden Centre Plc.

'Gardening Scotland' 2 -4 June 2006.
SGS and Dobbies Garden Centre Team.

Kibble Palace, Glasgow 25 November 2006.
Anniversary party given by our Glasgow Team. The anniversary cake.

Kibble Palace, Glasgow 25 November 2006.
Anniversary party given by our Glasgow Team.
Group of guests enjoying the celebrations.

Marine House Residential & Nursing Home, Rosemarkie.
One of the prize winners of the Queens Nursing Institute Scotland's
Gardening for Health Competition to mark the 75th Anniversary of SGS.

Our former Chairman, Mrs Robin Hunt and former Director, Mr Robin St. Clair-Ford who both retired at our AGM on 22 November 2006.

DUMFRIES

District Organiser: **Mrs Sarah Landale**, Dalswinton House, Dalswinton

Area Organiser: **Mrs Fiona Bell-Irving** Bankside, Kettleholm, Lockerbie.

Treasurer: **Mr J. Smith** Kirkmichael Old Manse, Parkgate, Dumfries DG1 3LY

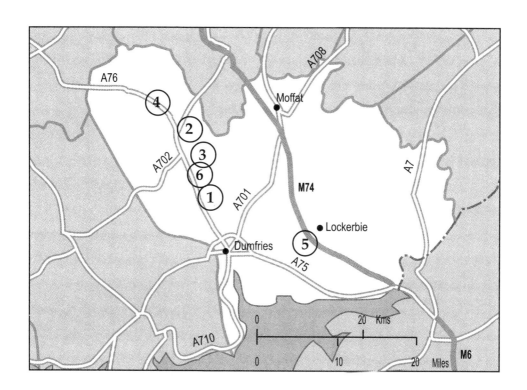

DATES OF OPENING

Portrack House, Holywood	Sunday 6 May	12 - 5pm
Dalswinton House, Auldgirth	Sunday 3 June	2 - 5pm
Cowhill Tower, Holywood	Sunday 1 July	2 - 5pm
Dabton, Thornhill	Sunday 8 July	2 - 5pm
Hallguards Riverside, Hoddam	Sunday 29 July	2 - 5pm
Enterkin Cottage, Dalswinton	Sunday 5 August	2 - 5pm

1. COWHILL TOWER, Holywood
(Captain & Mrs A E Weatherall)
Splendid views from lawn down Nith Valley. Interesting walled garden. Topiary animals, birds and figures. Woodland walk.
Route: Holywood 1½ miles off A76, 5 miles north of Dumfries.
Admission £3.00 Children £1.00
SUNDAY 1 JULY 2 - 5pm
40% to Macmillan Cancer Relief 60% net to SGS Charities

 (under cover) Produce stall

---

2. DABTON, Thornhill DG3 5AR
(The Earl and Countess of Dalkeith)
19th Century house built of pink stone. Extensive walled garden. Herbaceous border 95 yards long, roses, island beds and shrubs, ponds with azaleas and primulas. Woodland walk, vegetable garden, greenhouses.
Route: entrance off A76 between Thornhill and Carronbridge
Admission £3.00 Concession £2.00
SUNDAY 8 July 2 - 5pm
40% to Macmillan Cancer Support (Thornhill Committee) 60% net to SGS Charities

 (in old stables)

---

3. DALSWINTON HOUSE, Auldgirth DG2 0XZ
(Mr & Mrs Peter Landale)
Late C18 house sits on top of a hill surrounded by herbaceous beds and well established shrubs, including rhododendrons and azaleas. This overlooks the loch, which offers an attractive walk through woods and around the loch itself. It was here that the first steamboat in Britain made its maiden voyage in 1788 and there is a life-size model beside the water to commemorate this. There is a newly established plant centre in the old Walled Garden.
Route: Dumfries 7 miles off A76.
Admission £3.50 Children free
SUNDAY 3 JUNE 2 – 5pm
40% to Kirkmahoe Parish Church 60% net to SGS Charities

 (home-baked, at house)

---

4. ENTERKIN COTTAGE, Dalswinton DG2 0XZ **NEW**
(Martin McGrail)
New cottage garden being developed by the present owners. One acre of garden divided into vegetable and cottage gardens.
Route: between Thornhill and Sanquar on the A76.
Admission £3.00 Children 50p
SUNDAY 5 AUGUST 2 - 5pm
40% to Golden Retriever Rescue 60% net to SGS Charities

---

5. HALLGUARDS RIVERSIDE, Hoddam DG11 1AS

(Dai and Morag Griffiths)

Riverside (Annan) garden of about 2 acres of former Hoddam Estate Farmhouse, believed to be site of original Hoddam Castle. Yew trees to 800 years of age and wide variety of shrubs and herbaceous species.

<u>Route:</u> Garden situated beside Hoddam Bridge.

<u>Admission</u> £3.00 Children 50p

SUNDAY 29 JULY 2 - 5pm

20% to Sargent Cancer Care for Children 20% to Ecclefechan Surgery 60% net to SGS Charities

---

6. PORTRACK HOUSE, Holywood DG2 0RW

(Charles Jencks)

Original 18th century manor house with Victorian addition; octagonal folly-library. Twisted, undulating landforms and terraces designed by Charles Jencks as 'The Garden of Cosmic Speculation'; lakes designed by Maggie Keswick; rhododendrons, large new greenhouse in a geometric Kitchen Garden of the Six Senses; Glengower Hill plantation and view; woodland walks with Nonsense Building (architect: James Stirling); Universe cascade and rail garden of the Scottish Worthies; interesting sculpture including that of DNA.

<u>Route:</u> Holywood 1½ miles off A76, five miles north of Dumfries.

<u>Admission</u> £6.00

SUNDAY 6 MAY 12 - 5pm

40% to Maggie's Centre, Western General Hospital, Edinburgh   60% net to SGS Charities

---

Our website, www.gardensofscotland.org, provides information on Scotland's Gardens Scheme and the gardens that open for us.

The site will be re-designed in the course of 2007

DUNBARTONSHIRE WEST

District Organiser:	**Mrs K Murray,** 7 The Birches, Shandon, Helensburgh G84 8HN
Area Organisers:	**Mrs J Christie,** Gartlea, Gartocharn G83 9LX
	Mrs R Lang, Ardchapel, Shandon, Helensburgh G84 8NP
	Mrs R Macaulay, Denehard, Garelochhead G84 0EL
	Mrs S Miller, 8 Laggary Park, Rhu G84 8LY
	Mrs J Theaker, 19 Blackhill Drive, Helensburgh G84 9AF
Treasurer:	**Mrs H Wands,** Lindowan, Rhu G84 8NH

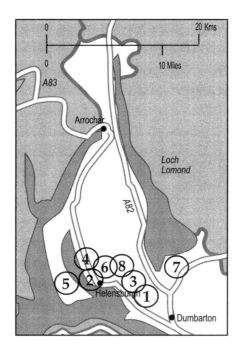

DATES OF OPENING

Glenarn, Rhu	21 March - 21 September Daily Sunrise - sunset	
Kilarden, Rosneath	Sunday 22 April	2 - 5pm
Geilston Garden, Cardross	Sunday 13 May	1 - 5pm
Ross Priory, Gartocharn	Sunday 20 May	2 - 5.30pm
East Bay Gardens, Helensburgh	Sunday 3 June	2 - 5pm
Cardross Gardens, Cardross	Sunday 10 June	2 - 5.30pm
Queen Street Gardens, Helensburgh	Sunday 24 June	2 - 5pm
Hill House Plant Sale, Helensburgh	Sunday 2 September	11am - 4pm

1. CARDROSS GARDENS, Cardross, Dumbarton G82 5EZ
Kirkton Cottage (Mr & Mrs T Duggan))
A garden of just less than one acre with mixed borders, shrubs, trees, herbs, vegetables, burn and pond.
High Auchensail (Mr and Mrs M Wilson)
A wild woodland rhododendron and azalea garden with tree house which has superb views over the Clyde.
Route: half mile and one mile respectively up Darleith Road off A814 at west end of Cardross village.
Admission £2.50 (includes both gardens) Children free
SUNDAY 10 JUNE 2 - 5.30pm
20% to Ardlui Respite Care Trust 20% to Christian Aid 60% net to SGS Charities

 (cream)

---

2. EAST BAY GARDENS, Helensburgh G82 7AX NEW
Most of the gardens of the Burgh's historic houses are hidden from public view. Opening for the first time this year are;
Tign-na-Mara, 152 East Clyde Street (Gordon and Kate Bennet) once the home of playwright, James Bridie, is set in approx. 1.5 acres. The garden construction began in 1990 and consists of mixed borders, rose garden, raised beds, patio areas and a sunken garden. Because of the somewhat unforgiving site, only metres from the Clyde, planting has had to be more a question of trial and error and survival of the fittest!
Rockland Coach House, 150 East Clyde Street (Net Lawrence) a secluded coach house garden with charming 'old world' atmosphere, incorporating some unusual features and interesting planting.
Cromalt, 148 East Clyde Street (Joan Robertson) at one time home to the novelist Neil Munro. The sweeping lawns overlooking the water and wide borders containing many of the original trees and shrubs give this fine house an air of period elegance.
Route: north on A814 from Dumbarton. At Helensburgh, immediately after crossing over hump-back railway bridge, all 3 houses stand together on left hand side. On-street parking.
Admission £3.00 includes all gardens Children free
SUNDAY 3 JUNE 2 - 5pm
40% to Macmillan Nurses 60% net to SGS Charities

 (limited)

---

3. GEILSTON GARDEN, Cardross G82 5HD
(The National Trust for Scotland)
The present design of Geilston Garden was laid out over 200 years ago to enhance Geilston House, which dates back to the late 17th century. The garden has many attractive features including the walled garden wherein a notable specimen of *Sequioadendron giganteum* dominates the lawn and the herbaceous border provides summer colour on a grand scale. In addition a wide range of fruit, vegetables and cut flowers is still cultivated in the kitchen garden. The Geilston Burn winds its way through enchanting woodland walks which provide spring displays of bluebells and azaleas.
Route: A814, Cardross 1 mile.
Admission £3.00 Children under 12 free
SUNDAY 13 MAY 1 - 5pm
40% to The Gardens Fund of The National Trust for Scotland 60% net to SGS Charities

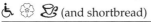 (and shortbread)

4. GLENARN, Rhu, Dunbartonshire G84 8LL
(Michael & Sue Thornley)
Sheltered woodland garden overlooking the Gareloch, famous for its collection of rare and tender rhododendrons, together with fine magnolias and other interesting trees and shrubs. Beneath are snowdrops, crocus, daffodils, erythroniums and primulas in abundance. Unfortunately work still continues in the rock garden (a long project) and there are beehives near the vegetable patch. Collection box, cars to be left at gate unless passengers are infirm.
Route: on A814, two miles north of Helensburgh.
Minimum donation £3.00 Children and concessions £1.50
21 MARCH - 21 SEPTEMBER DAILY Sunrise - sunset
Donation to Scotland's Gardens Scheme

🐕 ✿ (and honey for sale at times)

5. KILARDEN, Rosneath, Dumbartonshire G84 0PU
(Mr & Mrs J E Rowe)
Sheltered, hilly 10 acre woodland with notable collection of species and hybrid rhododendrons collected over a period of 50 years by the late Neil and Joyce Rutherford. Paths may be muddy.
Route: ¼ mile from Rosneath off B833 .
Admission to Garden £2.00 Children free
SUNDAY 22 APRIL 2 - 5pm
40% to Friends of St Modan's, Rosneath   60% net to SGS Charities

🐕 ✿ ☕ (in the village church hall)

6. QUEEN STREET GARDENS, Helensburgh G84 9LG `NEW`
The Old Coach House, 22 Queen Street (David and Maureen Morton)
The Glen, 24 Queen Street (Angus and Sophie Hamilton)
High Glenan, 24a Queen Street (Tom and Tricia Stewart)
Interesting group of neighbouring gardens offering a contrast of styles, old and new and reclaimed. Wooded area with burn and waterside plants; formal and courtyard gardens, gravel garden, alpine beds and area for reflection; fruit and vegetables.
Route: gardens are situated in West Helensburgh, approx. half-a-mile along Queen Street from its junction with Sinclair Street, on right hand side.
Admission £3.00 (includes all three gardens) Children welcome (under 12 free) though must be supervised at all times.
SUNDAY 24 JUNE 2 - 5pm
40% to Helensburgh Stroke Club 60% net to SGS Charities

♿ (mostly) ✿ ☕

7. ROSS PRIORY Gartocharn G83 8NL
(University of Strathclyde)
1812 Gothic addition by James Gillespie Graham to house of 1693 overlooking Loch Lomond. Rhododendrons, azaleas, selected shrubs and trees. Walled garden with glasshouses, pergola, ornamental plantings. Family burial ground. Nature and garden trails. House not open to view.
<u>Route:</u> Gartocharn 1½ miles off A811. Bus: Balloch to Gartocharn leaves Balloch at 1 pm and 3 pm.
<u>Admission</u> £3.00 Children free
SUNDAY 20 MAY 2 - 5.30pm
40% to CHAS 60% net to SGS Charities

  (in house) Putting green

PLANT SALE

8. HILL HOUSE, Helensburgh G84 9AJ
(The National Trust for Scotland)
Scotland's Gardens Scheme's Plant Sale is held in the garden of The Hill House, which has fine views over the Clyde estuary and is considered Charles Rennie Mackintosh's domestic masterpiece. The gardens continue to be restored to the patron's planting scheme with many features that reflect Mackintosh's design.
<u>Admission</u>: Plant Sale - free. Donations to SGS welcome
       House (1.30 - 5.30pm) - normal entrance charges. Possible restrictions.
SUNDAY 2 SEPTEMBER 11am - 4pm
40% to The Gardens Fund of the National Trust for Scotland 60% net to SGS Charities

♿ (gardens only) (tea room open from 11am)

> # GARDENING TIP
>
> Think about repotting before planting in a terracotta pot, especially plants that like to be pot bound. eg agapanthus. These can be impossible to remove from a pot if the top edge of the pot is one that tilts inwards.

EAST LOTHIAN

District Organiser: **The Lady Sarah Ward,** Stobshiel House, Humbie EH36 5PD
Tel: 01875 833646

Area Organisers: **Mrs C Gwyn,** The Walled Garden, Tyninghame,
Dunbar EH42 1XW
Mrs Carole Forbes, Hilltop Cottage, Hill Road, Gullane, East
Lothian EH31 2BE
Mr T W Jackson, Highbury, Whim Road, Gullane, East Lothian
EH31 2BD
Mrs W M C Kennedy, Oak Lodge, Inveresk, Musselburgh
EH21 7TE
Mrs N Parker, Steading Cottage, Stevenson, Haddington EH41 4PU

Treasurer: **Mr S M Edington,** Meadowside Cottage, Strathearn Road,
North Berwick EH39 5BZ

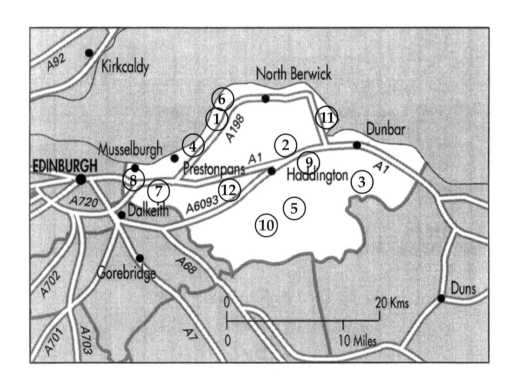

DATES OF OPENING

Inwood, Carberry .... 1 April - 30 September Tues, Thurs &
                                                        Sat 2 - 5pm
                                                        Groups by appt. Tel: 0131 665 4550
Shepherd House, Inveresk .... 17 April - 28 June Tues & Thurs 2 - 4pm
                                                        Groups by appt. Tel: 0131 665 2570
Stobshiel House, Humbie .... By appointment Tel: 01875 833646 or
                                                        e-mail: wardhersey@aol.com

Winton House, Pencaitland .... Sunday 1 April	12.30 - 4.30pm
Shepherd House, Inveresk .... Sunday 13 May	2 - 5pm
Tyninghame House, Dunbar .... Sunday 13 May	1 - 5pm
Clint, Stenton .... Sunday 20 May	2 - 5pm
Greywalls Hotel, Gullane .... Sunday 27 May	2 - 5pm
Athelstaneford Village, ... Sunday 3 June	2 - 6pm
Aberlady Village Gardens, ... Sunday 10 June	2 - 5pm
Gifford Bank and Broadwoodside, Gifford .... Sunday 17 June	2 - 5pm
Tyninghame House, Dunbar .... Sunday 24 June	1 - 5pm
Stevenson House & Walled Garden, Haddington Sunday 1 July	2 - 5pm
Inwood, Carberry .... Sunday 15 July	2 - 5pm
Community Gardens of Cockenzie & Port Seton Sunday 12 August	2 - 5pm

1. ABERLADY VILLAGE GARDENS EH32 0SB
A collection of diverse gardens within walking distance in the village of Aberlady.
Tickets from open gardens.
<u>Admission</u> £3.50   (Includes all gardens) Children free
<u>Route:</u> on A198 between Longniddry & Gullane.
SUNDAY 10 JUNE 2 - 5pm
All to SGS Charities

♿ (mostly) (in the Community Hall)

2. ATHELSTANEFORD VILLAGE EH39 5BE NEW
A variety of interesting village gardens of historical interest all within walking distance.
<u>Route:</u> B1343
<u>Admission</u> £3.00, children free, to all open gardens.
SUNDAY 3 JUNE 2 - 6pm
20% to Church Fund 20% to Village Hall Fund 60% net to SGS Charities

♿ (some)

3. CLINT, Stenton, Nr. Dunbar EH42 1TQ
(Mr & Mrs John W Blair)
Rhododendrons in woodland setting, herbaceous and primulas. Good for children.
<u>Route:</u> East Linton 3 miles, Stenton $^1/_2$ mile. South on the A1 turn right at East Linton.
After 2 miles turn right B6370 to Gifford. Drive entrance on left, exit through fields.
<u>Admission</u> £3.00 Children under 12 free
SUNDAY 20 MAY 2 - 5pm
40% to Save the Children 60% net to SGS Charities

4. THE COMMUNITY GARDENS OF COCKENZIE NEW
AND PORT SETON EH32 0AR
(East Lothian Council)
Visit some of the unique award-winning community gardens in Cockenzie and Port Seton. Each one has been created by the local community and has its own special character and history. There is a woodland garden, 2 gardens with stunning herbaceous borders and seaside gardens with planting appropriate for their exposed sites. All of the gardens are maintained by the local 'In Bloom' group and are within walking distance of each other. A descriptive leaflet and map will be made available at the Nursery Garden.
Route: FirstBus no. 129 (66 on a Sunday). Car - travel east along the B1348. Turn right immediately before Chalmers Church (the church with the spire in the middle of the village) into Osborne Terrace. Enter the school grounds which are approx. 100metres up on the right. Meet at the Nursery Garden in the grounds of Cockenzie Primary School.
Admission £2.50 Children free Families £5.00 OAP's £2.00
SUNDAY 12 AUGUST 2 - 5pm
40% to Macmillan Cancer Support 60% net to SGS Charities

 John Muir walkway links two harbours

5. GIFFORD BANK with BROADWOODSIDE, Gifford
Gifford Bank EH41 4JE
(Mr & Mrs Mark Hedderwick)
Walled garden filled with herbaceous, shrubs and vegetables. Greenhouses and frames plus two acres of informal garden of mature trees.
Broadwoodside, Gifford EH41 4JE
(Mr & Mrs Robert Dalrymple)
Recently featured in 'House & Garden'. A young garden planted in and around the courtyard of a converted farm steading, rescued from dereliction in 2000. Pond, temple and other follies in the surrounding farmland.
Route: on B6355 going out of Gifford towards the Golf Course.
Admission £4.50 (includes both gardens) Children under 12 free
SUNDAY 17 JUNE 2 - 6pm
40% to Cancer Research UK 60% net to SGS Charities

 (at Gifford Bank) (in the oak beamed hall at Broadwoodside)

6. GREYWALLS HOTEL, Gullane EH31 2EG
(Mr & Mrs Giles Weaver)
Six acres of formal garden attributed to Gertrude Jekyll complements the Edwardian house built by Sir Edwin Lutyens in 1901. Formal garden, herbaceous, shrub and annual borders.
Admission £3.00 Accompanied children free
SUNDAY 27 MAY 2 - 5pm
40% to Sick Kids Friends Fund 60% net to SGS Charities

7. INWOOD, Carberry EH21 8PZ
(Mr & Mrs I Morrison)
The one acre garden at Inwood is now over 20 years old and the roses, shrubs and trees have matured to provide the backdrop to colourful perennials, biennials, bulbs and annuals. This year's opening has been chosen to reflect the garden at peak season. RHS Partnership Garden.
Route: 1 mile south of Whitecraig on A6124.
Admission £3.00   Accompanied children free
SUNDAY 15 JULY 2 - 5.30pm
All takings to Scotland's Gardens Scheme

  ♿ *(with help)* ❀ ☕
Garden also open 1 April - 30 September Tuesday, Thursday & Saturday 2-5pm
Groups welcome by appointment Telephone: 0131 665 4550
E-mail : lindsay@inwoodgarden.com   Website: www.inwoodgarden.com

---

8. SHEPHERD HOUSE, Inveresk, near Musselburgh EH21 7TH
(Sir Charles & Lady Fraser)
Shepherd House and its one-acre garden form a walled triangle in the middle of the 18th century village of Inveresk. The main garden is to the rear of the house, where the formality of the front garden is continued with a herb parterre and two symmetrical potagers. A formal rill runs the length of the garden, beneath a series of rose, clematis and wistaria pergolas and arches, and connects the two ponds. The formality is balanced by the romance of the planting. Ann Fraser is an artist and the garden provides much of her inspiration.
Admission £3.00   Children free
SUNDAY 13 MAY 2 - 5pm
40% to Mercy Corps Scotland 60% net to SGS Charities
Also from 17 April until 28 June Tuesday & Thursday 2-4pm.
Groups welcome by appointment Telephone 0131 665 2570
E-mail annfraser@talktalk.net Website www.shepherdhousegarden.co.uk

---

9. STEVENSON HOUSE & THE WALLED GARDEN, Haddington EH41 4PU
Two different gardens with a variation on planting.
Stevenson House
(Mr and Mrs Ray Green)
A well established garden with a new rose garden, lime walk, large herbaceous borders and new borders planted around the magnificent house. An oak tree planted in 1560.
The Walled Garden
(Mr and Mrs Nicholas Parker)
Herbaceous centre walk, rose beds, large collection of hostas, gazebo garden, riverside and woodland walks.
Route: Two miles east of Haddington on the road to Hailes Castle.
Admission £3.00 Children under 12 free.
SUNDAY 1 JULY 2 – 5pm
40% to Childline 60% net to SGS Charities

10. STOBSHIEL HOUSE, Humbie EH36 5PD
(Mr Maxwell and Lady Sarah Ward)
Recently featured in 'Country Life', 'Scottish Field' and 'Scotland on Sunday'. A large
garden to see for all seasons. Walled garden adjacent to the house, box-edged
borders filled with herbaceous plants, bulbs, roses and lavender beds. Rustic
summerhouse. Glasshouse. Shrubbery with rhododendrons, azaleas and bulbs.
Water garden with meconopsis and primulas. Formal lily pond. Woodland walks.
Route: B6368 Haddington/Humbie roadsign to Stobshiel 1 mile.
Admission £3.00 Children under 12 free
OPEN BY APPOINTMENT Tel. 01875 833646 or E-mail:<u>wardhersey@aol.com</u>
40% to Family Service Unit Scotland 60% net to SGS Charities

11. TYNINGHAME HOUSE, Dunbar EH42 1XW
(Tyninghame Gardens Ltd)
Splendid 17th century pink sandstone Scottish baronial house, remodelled in 1829 by
William Burn, rises out of a sea of plants. Herbaceous border, formal rose garden,
Lady Haddington's secret garden with old fashioned roses, formal walled garden with
sculpture and yew hedges. The 'wilderness' spring garden with magnificent
rhododendrons, azaleas, flowering trees and bulbs. Grounds include one mile beech
avenue to sea, famous 'apple walk', Romanesque ruin of St Baldred's Church, views
across parkland to Tyne estuary and Lammermuir Hills.
Route: Tyninghame 1 mile.
Admission £3.50 OAP's £2.50 Children under 12 free
SUNDAYS 13 MAY & 24 JUNE 1 - 5pm
40% to John Muir Trust 60% net to SGS Charities

12. WINTON HOUSE, Pencaitland EH34 5AT
(Sir Francis Ogilvy Winton Trust)
The Gardens have been substantially improved and extended in recent years
extending down to Sir David's Loch and up into the walled garden. In Spring there is a
glorious covering of daffodils and other colours making way for the cherry and apple
blossoms.
Route: entrance off B6355 Tranent/Pencaitland road.
Admission: Grounds & café only: £2.50
House tour & grounds: £5.00, OAPs £4.00, children under 16 free
SUNDAY 1 APRIL 12.30 - 4.30pm
The Princess Royal Trust for Carers 60% net to SGS Charities

 (lunch, excellent home baking and afternoon teas)

PLANT SALE

13. SGS PLANT SALE - Joint opening East Lothian & Midlothian
held undercover at OXENFOORD MAINS, Near Pathhead EH22 2PF
Excellent selection of garden and house plants donated from private gardens.
Route: signed off A68, 4 miles south of Dalkeith.
Contact telephone number: Mrs Parker 01620 824788, Hon Michael Dalrymple 01875
320844 (office hours) or Mrs Barron 0131 663 1895.
SATURDAY 13 OCTOBER 9am- 2.30pm
40% to Cancer Research UK   60% net to SGS Charities

♿ ⛾ refreshments, home baking, fresh produce

EDINBURGH & WEST LOTHIAN

Joint District Organisers: **Mrs Victoria Reid Thomas,** Riccarton Mains Farmhouse, Currie EH14 4AR

Mrs Charles Welwood, Kirknewton House, Kirknewton, West Lothian EH27 8DA

Treasurer: **Mrs Charles Welwood,** Kirknewton House, Kirknewton, West Lothian EH27 8DA

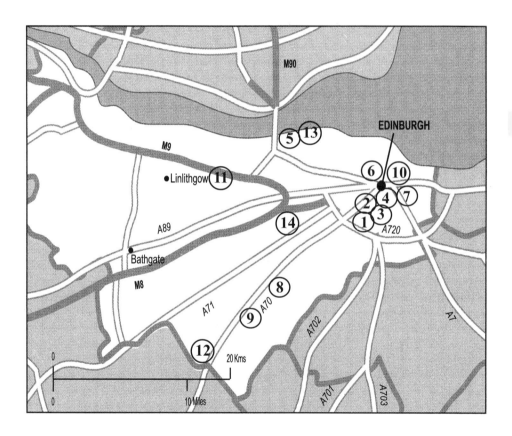

DATES OF OPENING

61 Fountainhall Road, Edinburgh .... By appointment Tel: 0131 667 6146
Newliston, Kirkliston .... 2 May - 3 June Wed - Sun 2 - 6pm

Dalmeny Park, South Queensferry (Snowdrops)	To be announced	
61 Fountainhall Road, Edinburgh	Sunday 8 April	2 - 5pm
61 Fountainhall Road, Edinburgh	Sunday 15 April	2 - 5pm
Dean Gardens, Edinburgh	Sunday 13 May	2 - 5pm
61 Fountainhall Road, Edinburgh	Sunday 20 May	2 - 5pm
61 Fountainhall Road, Edinburgh	Sunday 27 May	2 - 5pm
Suntrap Horticultural Centre, Edinburgh	Sunday 27 May	10.30am - 4.30pm
Sawmill, Harburn	Saturday 9 June	11am - 5pm
Moray Place & Bank Gardens, Edinburgh	Sunday 10 June	2 - 5pm
Malleny Garden, Balerno	Saturday 7 July	2 - 5pm
36 Morningside Drive, Edinburgh	Sunday 8 July	2 - 5pm
9 Braid Farm Road, Edinburgh	Sat & Sun 14 & 15 July	2 - 5pm
15 Morningside Park, Edinburgh	Sunday 15 July	2 - 5pm
Lymphoy House, Currie	Sunday 22 July	2 - 5pm
Dr Neil's Garden, Duddingston	Sat & Sun 4 & 5 August	2 - 5pm
South Queensferry Gardens.	Sunday 12 August	2 - 5pm
61 Fountainhall Road, Edinburgh	Sunday 2 September	2 - 5pm
61 Fountainhall Road, Edinburgh	Sunday 9 September	2 - 5pm
61 Fountainhall Road, Edinburgh	Sunday 7 October	2 - 5pm

1. 9 BRAID FARM ROAD, Edinburgh EH10 6LG
(Mr & Mrs R Paul)
A medium sized town garden of different styles. Cottage garden with pond.
Mediterranean courtyard and colourful decked area with water feature and exotic plants.
Mosaics and unusual features throughout.
Route: near Braid Hills Hotel, on the 11 and 15 bus routes.
Admission £3.00 Children free
SATURDAY & SUNDAY 14 & 15 JULY 2 - 5pm
40% to CHAS 60% net to SGS Charities

2. 15 MORNINGSIDE PARK, Edinburgh EH10 5HD
(Miller / Williams family)
Tiny town garden crammed with a variety of plants and interesting features,
including a Mediterranean-style patio and water feature.
Route: turn west off Morningside Road. On bus routes 11, 15, 16, 17, 5, 23, 41
Admission £3.00 Children free
SUNDAY 15 JULY
40% to The Citizen's Income Trust 60% net to SGS Charities
Cold drinks and biscuits

3. 36 MORNINGSIDE DRIVE, Edinburgh EH10 5LZ
(Mrs Elizabeth Casciani)
Private Victorian walled garden (85ft. x 45ft). Owner aims for year-round colour with
shrubs, roses and herbaceous planting. There are small fruit trees, fruit bushes and
tubs of various vegetables.
Admission £3.00 Children free
SUNDAY 8 JULY 2 - 5pm
40% between Water Aid & The Drum Riding for the Disabled 60% net to SGS Charities

4. 61 FOUNTAINHALL ROAD, Edinburgh EH9 2LH

(Dr J A & Mrs A Hammondl)

Large walled town garden in which trees and shrubs form an architectural backdrop to a wide variety of flowering plants. The growing collection of hellebores and trilliums and a large variety of late blooming flowers provide interest from early March to late October. In addition there are now several alpine beds which include a large collection of Sempervivums. Three ponds, with and without fish, have attracted a lively population of frogs.

Admission £3.00 Children free Parties welcome

SUNDAYS 8 & 15 APRIL, 20 & 27 MAY, 2 & 9 SEPTEMBER & 7 OCTOBER 2 - 5pm
Also by appointment. Tel: 0131 667 6146 or e-mail froglady@blueyonder.co.uk
40% to Froglife   60% net to SGS Charities

---

5. DALMENY PARK, South Queensferry EH30 9TQ

(The Earl & Countess of Rosebery)

Acres of snowdrops on Mons Hill. Paths can be slippy so please wear sensible footwear with good grip.

Route: South Queensferry, off A90 road to B924. Pedestrians and cars enter by Leuchold Gate and exit by Chapel Gate.

Admission £3.00 Children under 14 free

DATE TO BE ANNOUNCED
40% to St Columba's Hospice 60% net to SGS Charities

⛳ (in the Courtyard Tearoom, Dalmeny House)

---

6. DEAN GARDENS, Edinburgh EH4 1PJ

(Dean Gardens Management Committee)

Privately owned town gardens on north bank of the Water of Leith. 13½ acres of spring bulbs, daffodils and shrubs with lovely views over the Dean Valley. The Victorian pavilion has been reinstated and there is new seating throughout the garden.

Route: entrance at Ann Street or Eton Terrace.

Admission £2.50 Children free

SUNDAY 13 MAY 2 - 5pm
40% to the Gardens Fund of the National Trust for Scotland   60% net to SGS Charities
New members welcome to Dean Gardens.

---

7. DR NEIL'S GARDEN, Duddingston Village EH8 7DG

(Dr Neil's Garden Trust)

Landscaped garden on the lower slopes of Arthur's Seat using conifers, heathers and alpines.

Route: Car Park on Duddingston Road West.

Admission £2.50 Children free.

SATURDAY & SUNDAY 4 & 5 AUGUST 2 - 5pm
40% to Dr Neil's Garden Trust 60% net to SGS Charities

 (in Kirk Hall) book stall, children's activities

---

8. LYMPHOY HOUSE, Currie EH14 6AJ

(Roy & Doreen Mitchell)

Informal parkland garden with herbaceous borders, shrubbery and specimen trees. Pond and ruin of Lennox Tower. Kitchen garden, stables and woodland walks.

Route: A70 to Currie. Turn off into Kirkgate. Right along estate road (opposite graveyard gate). Half a mile on, park at bollards.

Admission £3.00 Children free

SUNDAY 22 JULY 2 - 5pm

40% to Special Needs Information Point 60% net to SGS Charities

 wine

---

9. MALLENY GARDEN, Balerno EH14 7AF

(National Trust for Scotland)

3 acre walled garden with 17th century clipped yew trees, lawns & borders. Wide & varied selection of herbaceous plants & shrubs. Shrub roses including NCCPG 19th century rose collection, ornamental vegetable & herb garden. Greenhouse display.

Route: in Balerno, off A70 Lanark Road. LRT No. 44   First Bus No. 44.

Admission £3.00 Children £2.00

SATURDAY 7 JULY 2 - 5pm

40% to NTS Gardens Fund 60% net to SGS Charities

10.MORAY PLACE & BANK GARDENS, Edinburgh EH3 6BX

Moray Place

Private garden of $3^1/2$ acres in Georgian New Town, recently benefitted from five-year programme of replanting; shrubs, trees and beds offering atmosphere of tranquility in the city centre.

Entrance: north gate in Moray Place.

Bank Gardens

Nearly six acres of secluded wild gardens with lawns, trees and shrubs with banks of bulbs down to the Water of Leith; stunning vistas across Firth of Forth.

Entrance: gate at top of Doune Terrace.

Admission £2.50 Children free

SUNDAY 10 JUNE 2 - 5pm

40% to Marie Curie Cancer Care 60% net to SGS Charities

---

11. NEWLISTON, Kirkliston EH29 9EB

(Mr & Mrs R C Maclachlan)

18th century designed landscape. Rhododendrons and azaleas. The house, which was designed by Robert Adam, is open. On Sundays there is a ride-on steam model railway from 2 - 5 pm.

Route: four miles from Forth Road Bridge, entrance off B800.

Admission to House & Garden £2.50 Children & OAPs £1.50

2 MAY - 3 JUNE WEDNESDAY - SUNDAY 2 - 6pm

40% to Children's Hospice Association Scotland 60% net to SGS Charities

 steam model railway

---

12. SAWMILL, Harburn EH55 8RE

(Andrew Leslie)

Valley garden built around the ruins of an old water mill. Mixed planting, including herbaceous and bog gardens, with azaleas and asiatic primulas. The garden is open in conjunction with the Harburn Festival.

Route: A70 Edinburgh/Lanark road, or A71 to West Calder, then B7008.

Admission £2.50 Children under 15 Free

SATURDAY 9 JUNE 11am - 5pm

40% to Harburn Village Hall 60% net to SGS Charities

 ❀ ☕ (in Community Hall)

Harburn Festival (crafts, art exhibition, dog show, bouncy castle, etc)

---

13. SOUTH QUEENSFERRY GARDENS EH30 9HY

A group of gardens of varied size and design, with many surprises, in the historic town of South Queensferry. Tickets and maps available on the day from **St. Mary's House, Kirkliston Road, South Queensferry** and **The Forts, Hawes Brae, South Queensferry.**

Route: off A90, north of Edinburgh.

Admission £3.00

SUNDAY 12 AUGUST 2 - 5pm

40% to Care in the Community 60% net to SGS Charities

☕

---

14. SUNTRAP EDINBURGH HORTICULTURAL & GARDENING CENTRE, Gogarbank, Edinburgh EH13 0PB

(Oatridge Agricultural College, organised by Friends of Suntrap Edinburgh NTS Members Centre)

A horticultural out-centre of Oatridge College. Compact garden of 1.7 hectares (3 acres), range of areas including rock and water features, sunken garden, raised beds, vegetable zone, sensory garden, woodland plantings & greenhouses. New home of the Scottish Bonsai Collection. Facilities for professional and amateur instruction, meeting and classroom facilities, horticultural advice and visitor interest.

Route: signposted 0.5m west of Gogar roundabout, off A8 and 0.25m west of Calder Junction (City bypass) off A71. Bus route: Mactours No. 67. Parking for disabled drivers inside main gate; other parking opposite.

Admission £2.50 Children & OAPs £1.50

SUNDAY 27 MAY 10.30am - 4.30pm

20% to Perennial (GRBS) 20% to Friends of Suntrap   60% net to SGS Charities

♿ ❀ ☕ (home baked) Family day out with horticultural advice surgery, stalls and entertainment.

Open daily throughout the year until dusk with same facilities.

Friends of Suntrap Edinburgh programme of events - www.ntscentres.org.uk/suntrap. Advice/booking Tel: 0131 339 7283.

ETTRICK & LAUDERDALE

District Organiser:	**Mrs D Muir**, Torquhan House, Stow TD1 2RX
Area Organiser:	**Mrs M Kostoris,** Wester Housebyres, Melrose TD6 9BW
Treasurer:	**Mr Miller,** 18 Craigpark Gardens, Galashiels TD1 3HZ

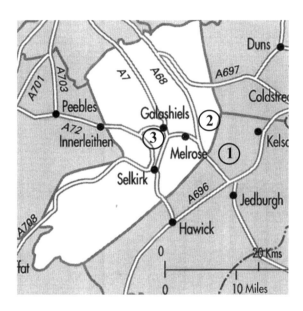

DATES OF OPENING

Bemersyde, Melrose	Sunday 22 April	2 - 5pm
Fairnilee House, ...	Sunday 8 July	2 - 5pm
Carolside, Earlston	Saturday 14 July	2 - 6pm

1. BEMERSYDE, Melrose TD6 9DP
(The Earl Haig)
16th century peel tower reconstructed in the 17th century with added mansion house. Garden laid out by Field Marshal Earl Haig. Views of Eildon Hills. Woodland garden and river walks. Admission to garden only.
Route: B6356 St Boswells via Clintmains or Melrose via Leaderfoot Bridge.
Admission £3.00 Children under 10 free
SUNDAY 22 APRIL 2 - 5pm
40% to Lady Haig's Poppy Factory 60% net to SGS Charities

2. CAROLSIDE, Earlston TD4 6AL

(Mr & Mrs Anthony Foyle)
18th century house set in parkland. A very traditional elliptical walled garden with a beautiful collection of old roses and herbaceous border. Herb garden, oval rose garden and mixed borders.
Route: turn off A68 at sign one mile north of Earlston, six miles south of Lauder.
Admission £3.50 Children free
SATURDAY 14 JULY 2 - 6pm
20% to British Red Cross 20% to RNLI 60% net to SGS Charities

---

3. FAIRNILEE HOUSE, NEW

(Mr and Mrs Mason)
Mature extensive gardens that have been beautifully restored over past 4 years having been totally neglected for 40 years previously, surrounding impressive family house; woodland, orchard, shrubs, herbaceous borders, parterre and stunning rose arbours, allees and terraces. Greenhouses.
Route: on A708 between Caddonfoot and Yair, turn off A7 to Yair between Galashiels and Selkirk.
Admission TBC
SUNDAY 8 JULY 2 - 5pm
40% to William Thyne Trust (Cancer) 60% net to SGS Charities

GARDENING TIP

To prevent squirrels and mice from stealing tulip and crocus bulbs cover planted bulbs with soil, then chicken wire before covering with remaining soil. This also works well with pots and containers.

FIFE

District Organiser:	**Mrs Catherine Erskine,** Cambo House, Kingsbarns KY16 8QD
Area Organisers:	**Mrs Jeni Auchinleck,** 2 Castle Street, Crail KY10 3SQ
	Mrs Evelyn Crombie, West Hall, Cupar KY15 4NA
	Mrs Nora Gardner, Inverie, 36 West End, St Monans KY10 2BX
	Mrs Gill Hart, Kirklands House, Saline KY12 9TS
	Mrs Kathleen Maxwell, Micklegarth, Aberdour KY3 9AS
	Mrs Lindsay Murray, Craigfoodie, Dairsie, Fife KY15 4RU
	Mrs Marilyn Whitehead, Greenside, Leven KY8 5NU
Plant Sale Organisers:	**Mrs Sue Eccles**, Whinhill, Upper Largo KY8 5QS
	Ms Louise Roger, Chesterhill, Boarhills, St Andrews KY16 8PP
Treasurer:	**Mrs Fay Smith,** 37 Ninian Fields, Pittenweem, Anstruther KY10 2QU

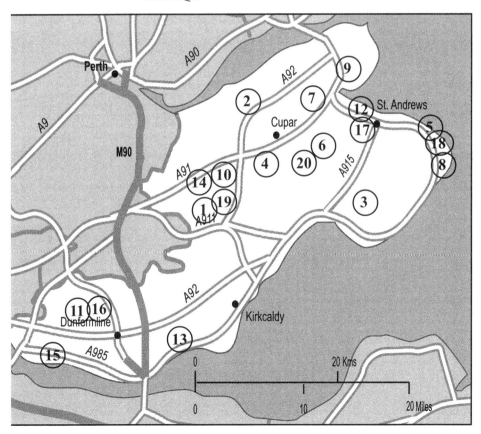

DATES OF OPENING

Barham, Bow of Fife	15 February - 30 September by appt.	
	Tel. 01337 810227	
Cambo, Kingsbarns	All year	10am - 5pm
Strathtyrum, St Andrews	June, August & September	
	Wednesday - Sunday	2 - 4pm
Cambo, Kingbarns (Spring plant/craft fair)	Sunday 29 April	12 - 4pm
Saline Village Gardens, Saline	Sunday 27 May	2 - 6pm
Earlshall Castle, Leuchars	Sunday 3 June	2 - 5pm
Micklegarth, Aberdour	Sunday 3 June	2 - 5pm
Arnot Tower & Greenhead of Arnot	Sunday 10 June	2 - 5pm
Aytounhill House, Newburgh	Sunday 10 June	11am - 5pm
Karbet, Freuchie (in conjunction with plant sale) ...	Saturday 16 June	Noon - 4pm
Aytounhill House, Newburgh	Sunday 24 June	11am - 5pm
Kirklands, Saline	Sunday 24 June	2 - 5pm
Aytounhill House, Newburgh	Sunday 1 July	11am - 5pm
Balcarres, Colinsburgh	Sunday 1 July	2 - 5.30pm
Myres Castle, by Auchtermuchty	Sunday 1 July	2 - 5pm
Earlshall Castle, Leuchars	Sunday 8 July	2 - 5pm
Wormistoune, Crail	Sunday 15 July	2 - 5.30pm
Crail: Small Gardens in the Burgh, ...	Sat & Sun 21 & 22 July	1 - 5.30pm
Craigfoodie, ...	Sunday 29 July	2 - 5pm
Ladies Lake, St Andrews	Sunday 19 August	2 - 5pm
Parleyhill Garden & Manse Garden, Culross.	Sunday 26 August	1- 5pm
Ceres Village Gardens, Cupar	Sunday 9 September	2 - 5pm
Cambo, Kingsbarns (Apple day)	Sunday 16 September	2 - 5pm
Falkland Palace, Falkland	Sunday 23 September	1 - 5pm
Karbet, Freuchie Plant Sale	Saturday 16 June	Noon - 4pm
Annual Plant Sale and Fair, Hill of Tarvit	Sunday 7 October	10.30 - 4.30pm

1. ARNOT TOWER & GREENHEAD OF ARNOT KY6 3JQ
Arnot Tower
(Benjamin & Helen Gray)
New formal garden and award-winning wedding venue created around the ruins of a 15th century tower. Herbaceous borders, terraces, tree rhododendrons. Long pool with fountains, views over Loch Leven.
Greenhead of Arnot
(Mr & Mrs M Strang Steel)
Newly created open garden surrounding renovated farmhouse with newly planted orchard, rose trellis, herbs and vegetables.
Route: A911 between Auchmuir Bridge and Scotlandwell.
Admission £3.50 for both gardens   Children free
SUNDAY 10 JUNE 2 - 5pm
40% to Mercy Ships 60% net to SGS Charities

2. AYTOUNHILL HOUSE, Newburgh KY14 6JH

(Mr Neil Findlay)

Several mixed borders with a wide variety of shrubs and herbaceous plants. Traditional vegetable garden. Splendid situation. Walk round loch and varieties of trees. New arboretum

<u>Route:</u> off A913, 7 miles from Cupar and Newburgh

<u>Admission</u> £3.50 Accompanied children free

SUNDAY 10 JUNE 11am - 5pm
SUNDAY 24 JUNE 11am - 5pm
SUNDAY 1 JULY 11am - 5pm

20% to Dunbog Village Hall 20% to Abdie Church 60% net to SGS Charities

 (and Soup 10 June - no refreshments served 24 June or 1 July)

3. BALCARRES, Colinsburgh KY9 1HL

(The Earl and Countess of Crawford and Balcarres)

19th Century formal and woodland garden; wide variety of plants.

<u>Route:</u> $^1/_2$ mile north of Colinsburgh off A942.

<u>Admission</u> £4.00 Accompanied children free

SUNDAY 1 JULY 2 - 5.30pm

20% to Maggie's Centre 20% to SWRI   60% net to SGS Charities

4. BARHAM, Bow of Fife KY15 5RG

(Sir Robert & Lady Spencer-Nairn)

A small woodland garden with rhododendrons, spring bulbs, trilliums and ferns. Also a summer garden with herbaceous borders and island beds.

<u>Route:</u> A91, 4 miles west of Cupar.

<u>Admission</u> £3.50 Children under 12 free

15 FEBRUARY - 30 SEPTEMBER BY APPOINTMENT TEL. 01337 810227

40% to Pain Association Scotland 60% net to SGS Charities

  (unusual plants)

5. CAMBO HOUSE, Kingsbarns KY16 8QD

(Peter & Catherine Erskine)

Romantic Victorian walled garden designed around the Cambo burn with willow, waterfall and charming wrought-iron bridges. Ornamental potager, breathtaking snowdrops (mail order in February) massed spring bulbs, lilac walk, naturalistic plantings, woodland garden, old roses, colchicum meadow and glowing autumn borders. All seasons plantsman's paradise. Woodland walks to the sea. Featured in 'Country Life' and 'The Garden'.

<u>Route:</u> A917.

<u>Admission</u> £3.50 Children free

SUNDAY 29 APRIL 12 - 4pm - Spring Plant and Craft Fair.

40% to Diabetes UK   60% net to SGS Charities

SUNDAY 16 SEPTEMBER 2 - 5pm - Apple day - bring apples, make your own juice, apple recipies to try and buy, toffee apples, apple 'dooking', apple doctor

All proceeds to SGS Charities

Also all year round 10am - 5pm

  (home made) Soup and rolls 29 April

6. CERES VILLAGE GARDENS, Cupar KY15 5YS NEW
(The gardeners of Ceres)
Ceres, often described as the most beautiful village in Scotland, can offer seven gardens in a variety of shapes and sizes. In addition, Fife Folk Museum and the Griselda Hill Wemyss Ware Pottery can be visited. A footbridge from Ceres car park leads directly into the Museum garden where tickets (maps indicating the gardens) can be purchased. From there, a pleasant stroll around the village includes all the gardens.
<u>Route:</u> map indicating gardens on entry at Museum garden which is adjacent to Ceres car park.
<u>Admission</u> £3.50 Acccompanied children free
SUNDAY 9 SEPTEMBER 2 - 5pm
40% Fife Folk Museum 60% net to SGS Charities

♿ (partly) Fife Folk Museum Griselda Hill Wemyss Ware Pottery

7. CRAIGFOODIE, Dairsie KY15 4RU NEW
(Mr & Mrs James Murray)
Recently restored formal walled garden adjoining 17th century house and enjoying fine aspect - parterres, clock lawn, mixed/herbaceous borders, dry mill, interestingly planted terrace and vegetable garden. Also newly created woodland garden.
<u>Route:</u> on A91 from Cupar to St Andrews turn left at Dairsie School, then follow signs.
<u>Admission</u> £3.50 Children free
SUNDAY 29 JULY 2 - 5pm
40% to Association for International Cancer Research (AICR) 60% net to SGS Charities

♿ (partly) (not in walled garden)

8. CRAIL: SMALL GARDENS IN THE BURGH KY10 3SQ
(The Gardeners of Crail)
A number of small gardens in varied styles: cottage, historic, plantsman's, bedding. Tickets and map available from Mrs Auchinleck, 2 Castle Street, Crail and Mr and Mrs Robertson, The Old House, 9 Marketgate. (Last tickets sold at 4.30pm)
<u>Route:</u> approach Crail from either St Andrews or Anstruther, A917. Park in the Marketgate.
<u>Admission</u> £3.50 Acccompanied Children free
SATURDAY & SUNDAY 21 & 22 JULY 1 - 5.30pm
20% to Crail British Legion Hall Fund 20% to Crail Preservation Society 60% net to SGS Charities

 (in the British Legion Hall)

9. EARLSHALL CASTLE, Leuchars KY16 0DP
(Paul & Josine Veenhuijzen)
Garden designed by Sir Robert Lorimer. Topiary lawn, for which Earlshall is renowned, rose terrace, croquet lawn with herbaceous borders, shrub border, box garden and orchard.
<u>Route:</u> on Earlshall Road 3/4 of a mile east of Leuchars Village (off A919).
<u>Admission</u> £5.00 Children free
SUNDAY 3 JUNE 2 - 5pm
40% to The Liberating Scots Trust   60% net to SGS Charities
SUNDAY 8 JULY 2 - 5.pm
40% to The Princess Royal Trust for Carers   60% net to SGS Charities

10. FALKLAND PALACE GARDEN, Falkland KY15 7BU

(The National Trust for Scotland)
The Royal Palace of Falkland, set in the heart of a medieval village, was the country residence and hunting lodge of eight Stuart monarchs, including Mary, Queen of Scots. The palace gardens were restored by the late Keeper, Major Michael Crichton Stuart, to a design by Percy Cane.
Route: A912.
Admission to Garden £5.00 Family ticket £12.50
For Palace admission prices and concessions please see the NTS advert at back of book
SUNDAY 23 SEPTEMBER 1 - 5pm
40% to The Gardens Fund of the National Trust for Scotland 60% net to SGS Charities

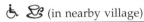 (in nearby village)

---

11. KIRKLANDS, Saline KY12 9TS

(Peter & Gill Hart)
Kirklands has been developed and restored over the last 30 years, although the house dates from 1832. Herbaceous borders, bog garden, woodland garden and walled garden (still being restored). Recently planted woodland area. Saline Burn divides the garden from the ancient woodland and the woodland walk.
Route: Junction 4, M90, then B914. Parking in the centre of the village.
Admission £3.00 Accompanied children free
SUNDAY 24 JUNE 2 - 5pm
40% to Saline Environmental Group 60% net to SGS Charities

 (partial) B&B

---

12. LADIES LAKE, The Scores, St Andrews KY16 9AR

(Mr and Mrs Gordon T Senior)
The garden is small, no more than half an acre. It occupies a saucer-shaped curve on the cliff adjacent to St Andrews Castle. In essence, the garden consists of two terraces, one of which is cantilevered over the sea. About 6,000 bedding plants are crammed into half a dozen beds.
Route: from North Street, turn left into North Castle Street, left in front of castle and house is 150 yards on right.
Admission £3.00 Accompanied children free
SUNDAY 19 AUGUST 2 - 5pm
40% to Hope Park Church, St Andrews 60% net to SGS Charities

(with help - some steps) (provided by the ladies of Hope Park Church)
Music

13. MICKLEGARTH, Aberlour KY3 0SW
(Mr and Mrs Gordon Maxwell)
Tucked away in what was once the back-lands of half a dozen High Street properties
in a historic coastal village. This gently-sloping, half-acre garden benefits from a
southern exposure and well-drained soils that have been worked for at least five
centuries. Its present appearance - an informal and densely planted blend of specimen trees and shrubs, herbaceous island-beds, roses and herbs, linked by winding
grassy paths - goes back to 1972, when the present owners restored it from a derelict
state and began to create a garden which, all year round, would provide pleasure,
interest and a warm personal welcome.
Route: off High Street in Aberlour.
Admission £3.00 Children under 10 free
SUNDAY 3 JUNE 2 - 5pm
40% to PDSA 60% net to SGS Charities

 (access restricted)

14. MYRES CASTLE, Auchtermuchty KY14 7EW
(Mr & Mrs Jonathan White)
Formal walled gardens laid out in the style of the Vatican gardens in Rome to reflect
the Fairlie family's papal connections.
Route: on the B936, off the A91
Admission £5.00
SUNDAY 1 JULY 2 - 5pm
40% to Rachel House Children's Hospice, Kinross 60% net to SGS Charities

 (gravel drive)   (and cake included in entry price)

15. PARLEYHILL GARDEN & MANSE GARDEN Culross KY12 8JD
(Mr & Mrs R J McDonald & Revd & Mrs T Moffat)
Overlooking the Forth and the historic village of Culross, both these gardens nestle in the
shade of Culross Abbey and the adjacent Abbey ruins. Parleyhill Garden has evolved in
two parts, the earlier in the mid 60s, the latter in the late 80's. The garden of the Abbey
Manse is situated in the old Abbey cloister garden. Both are delightful hidden gardens
bordered by stone walls with interesting displays of old fashioned herbaceous perennials
and a good variety of seasonal plants, bulbs and shrubs.
Route: A985 then follow signs to Culross. Parking at the Abbey and in the village.
Admission £3.00 Accompanied children free
SUNDAY 26 AUGUST 1 - 5pm
40% to Culross and Torryburn Church 60% net to SGS Charities

 (access to Parleyhill Garden and Manse tearoom)

16. SALINE VILLAGE GARDENS, Saline KY12 9LL
A number of varied styles and sizes of gardens from large established to recently
developed - from small cottage gardens to wooded sloping garden.
Route: junction 4 M90 then B914. Parking in the centre of the village near the bus
turning circle, where tickets and maps will be available.
Admission £4.50 Accompanied children free.
SUNDAY 27 MAY 2 - 6pm
20% to Saline Environmental Group 20% Saline Church 60% net to SGS Charities

 (in Church Hall)   Gallery   Children's treasure hunt

90

17. STRATHTYRUM, St Andrews KY16 9SF

(Mr and Mrs A Cheape)

Gardens surrounding house, including small rose garden and newly restored four acre walled garden.

<u>Route:</u> Large iron gates with grey urns on right of A91 - half mile before St Andrews on Guardbridge side.

<u>Admission</u> £3.00 (House open - Admission £5.00 Child £2.50)

JUNE, AUGUST & SEPTEMBER WEDNESDAY - SUNDAY 2 - 4pm

40% Maggie's Centre 60% net to SGS Charities

---

18. WORMISTOUNE, Crail KY10 3XH

(James & Gemma McCallum of Wormistoune)

17th century formal walled and woodland garden. New pleasance garden and mosaic celtic cross. Splendid herbaceous border. Largest listed Grisselinia in Scotland

<u>Route:</u> On A917 Crail - St Andrews.

<u>Admission</u> £4.00

SUNDAY 15 JULY 2 - 5.30pm

40% to Crail Parish Church 60% net to SGS Charities

GARDENS OPEN BY INVITATION ONLY

46 SOUTH STREET, St Andrews (Mrs June Baxter)

STRATHMORE COTTAGE, Drumeldrie (Willie Duncan & Miss Barbara Whitelaw)

These gardens will be opening in 2007 to invitation holders only.
If you would like to apply for an invitation please contact:

Mrs Lindsay Murray Tel. 01334 870291   e-mail: lindsaypmurray@btinternet.com
or Jeni Auchinleck Tel. 01333 450538

(FIFE PLANT SALES OVERLEAF)

PLANT SALES

19. FREUCHIE PLANT SALE at KARBET KY15 7EY
(Major & Mrs A B Cran)
A wide selection of plants: Perennial and bedding will be on sale at Karbet in the centre of Freuchie.
Route: is in the centre of Freuchie on the B936.
Admission £1.00 Children free
SATURDAY 16 JUNE Noon - 4pm
40% to SSAFA Forces Help   60% net to SGS Charities

♿ (with help) ☕ Refreshments.

---

20. ANNUAL SGS PLANT SALE AND FAIR HILL OF TARVIT, Cupar KY15 5PB
(The National Trust for Scotland)
Interesting selection of plants and clumps of herbaceous plants at bargain prices.
Route: A916.
SUNDAY 7 OCTOBER 10.30 - 4.30pm
40% to Homestart and East Neuk National Trust Gardens   60% net to SGS Charities

☕ (refreshments) Food and garden craft fair   Gardener's question time.

GLASGOW & DISTRICT

District Organiser: **Mrs V A Field,** Killorn, 8 Baldernock Road, Milngavie G62 8DR

Area Organisers: **Mrs A Barlow,** 5 Auchencruive, Milngavie G62 6EE
Mrs M Collins, Acre Valley House, Torrance G64 4DJ
Mrs C M T Donaldson, 2 Edgehill Road, Bearsden G61 3AD
Mr A Heasman, 76 Sandhead Terrace, Blantyre G72 0JH
Mrs A Murray, 44 Gordon Road, Netherlee G44 5TW
Mr Alan Simpson, 48 Thomson Drive, Bearsden G61 3NZ
Mrs A C Wardlaw, 92 Drymen Road, Bearsden G61 2SY

Treasurer: **Mr J Murray,** 44 Gordon Road, Netherlee G44 5TW

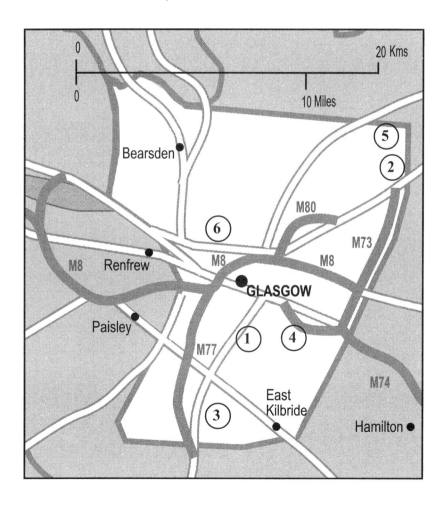

DATES OF OPENING

Invermay, Cambuslang .... April - Sept. groups by appt.
Tel. 0141 641 1632

122 Millersneuk Crescent, Millerston, Stepps ..... Sunday 13 May   2 - 5pm
Kilsyth Gardens. .... Sunday 20 May   2 - 5pm
44 Gordon Road, Netherlee .... Sunday 3 June   2 - 5pm
Hill of Birches, Waterfoot Row, Thornton Hall .. Sunday 19 August   2 - 5pm

Glasgow Botanic Gardens, Plant sale .... Saturday 9 June   11am - 4pm

1. 44 GORDON ROAD, Netherlee G44 5TW
(Anne & Jim Murray)
Mature town garden of approximately one acre containing large trees, rhododendrons and herbaceous borders with many unusual plants. A Japanese garden and water feature are among more recent developments. New garden sculptures. Garden as seen in 'Beechgrove Garden'.
Route: B767 Clarkston Road past Linn Park gates, turn at Williamwood Drive then second turning on the left.
Admission £3.00 Children free
SUNDAY 3 June 2 - 5pm
40% Erskine Hospital 60% net to SGS Charities

  Refreshments.

2. 122 MILLERSNEUK CRESCENT, Millerston, Stepps G33 6PH NEW
(Ian & Alison Doig)
A town garden with imaginative design features and a wide selection of plants. Trees, herbaceous plants, shrubs and bulbs combine to provide an eye catching mixture and a most interesting backdrop in a suburban setting.
Route: follow A80 Cumbernauld Road (eastbound) past Hogganfield Loch, turn left into Station Road (at traffic lights) and follow to the last junction on the right before the end of the road.
Admission £5.00 (includes tea and light refreshments)
SUNDAY 13 MAY 2 - 5pm
40% Craig Halbert School (Motor Neurone Disease) 60% net to SGS Charities

  (refreshments)

3. HILL OF BIRCHES, Waterfoot Row, Thornton Hall G74 5AD NEW
(Mr & Mrs Donald Storrie)
A fine garden developed over the last 20 years with a good selection of perennials, shrubs and mature trees in hedged enclosures surrounding the house. Extensive perimeter woodlands, with good views into steep valleys and over the surrounding countryside.
Route: take B767 Glasgow Road from Clarkston to Eaglesham. At Waterfoot, take care turning into Waterfoot Row, climb hill and follow signs.
Admission £3.00 Children over 12 £1.00
SUNDAY 19 AUGUST 2 - 5pm
40% Marie Curie Cancer Trust 60% net to SGS Charities

 (surplus) (light refreshments with home baking)

4. INVERMAY, 48 Wellshot Drive, Cambuslang G72 8BN

(Mrs M Robertson)
A plant lovers' garden. Wide variety of unusual bulbs, rock plants, herbaceous plants, shrubs (many named) in a very sheltered, suburban garden. Greenhouse with fuchsias. Something in flower all through the year - a special town garden.
Route: A730 (East Kilbride) or A749/A724 (Hamilton) from Glasgow. Convenient to M74/M73. Wellshot Drive starts at back of Cambuslang Station.
Admission £2.50 Children over 12 £1.00
APRIL - SEPTEMBER Groups by appointment, please telephone first: 0141 641 1632
40% to Children First 60% net to SGS Charities

---

5. KILSYTH GARDENS G65 9DE

Aeolia (Mr & Mrs G Murdoch)
Has a garden of a third of an acre developed since 1960 by the present owners and contains many mature specimen trees and shrubs, a large variety of rhododendrons, primulas, hardy geraniums and herbaceous plants.
Blackmill (Mr John Patrick)
Is on the opposite side of the road from Aeolia and has an acre of ground developed on the site of an old mill. Half of the garden has mature and recent plantings, an ornamental mill and pond with the other half consisting of a natural wood and a glen with a cascading waterfall.
Route: Take A803 to Kilsyth, turn northwards into Parkburn Road and then follow signs from top of hill.
Admission £5.00 includes both gardens and home made tea Children free
SUNDAY 20 MAY 2 - 5pm
40% to Strathcarron Hospice 60% net to SGS Charities

PLANT SALE

6. GLASGOW BOTANIC GARDENS G12 0UE

(Glasgow City Council)
Glasgow District's Annual Plant Sale will again be held in the spring. A large selection of indoor and outdoor plants and shrubs will be for sale. There will also be an opportunity to view the National Collection of Begonias and the extensive propogation areas. Scotland's largest collection of filmy ferns set in a fairy like grotto will also be open to view and this is particularly appealing to children.
Route: Leave M8 at Junction 17, follow signs for Dumbarton. The Botanic Garden is at the junction of Great Western Road A82 and Queen Margaret Drive.
Any donation of plants beforehand would be welcome: Please contact 0141 956 5478
Admission Free
SATURDAY 9 JUNE 11am - 4pm
25% to Friends of the Botanics   75% net to SGS Charities

 (refreshments)

ISLE OF ARRAN

District Organiser: **Mrs S C Gibbs,** Dougarie, Isle of Arran KA27 8EB

Treasurer: **Mr D Robertson,** Bank of Scotland, Brodick KA27 8AL

DATES OF OPENING

Dougarie.	Sunday 1 July	2 - 5pm
Brodick Castle & Country Park	Sunday 15 July	10am - 5pm
Brodick Castle & Country Park	Sunday 12 August	10am - 5pm

1. BRODICK CASTLE & COUNTRY PARK
(The National Trust for Scotland)
Exotic plants and shrubs. Walled garden. Woodland garden.
Route: Brodick 2 miles. Service buses from Brodick Pier to Castle. Regular sailings
from Ardrossan and from Claonaig (Argyll). Information from Caledonian MacBrayne,
Gourock. Tel: 01475 650100.
Admission to Garden & Country Park £5.00 Concessions £4.00
SUNDAYS 15 JULY & 12 AUGUST 10am - 5pm
40% to The Gardens Fund of the National Trust for Scotland   60% net to SGS Charities
 (some) ☕ NTS Shop

2. DOUGARIE
(Mr & Mrs S C Gibbs)
Terraced garden in castellated folly. Shrubs, herbaceous borders, traditional kitchen
garden.
Route: Blackwaterfoot 5 miles. Regular ferry sailing from Ardrossan and from
Claonaig (Argyll). Information from Caledonian MacBrayne, Gourock. Tel: 01475
650100.
Admission £2.50 Children free
SUNDAY 1 JULY 2 - 5pm
40% to an Island Charity   60% net to SGS Charities
☕ Produce stall

KINCARDINE & DEESIDE

District Organiser:	**Mrs D White**, Lys-na-greyne House, Aboyne AB34 5JD
Area Organisers:	**The Hon Mrs J K O Arbuthnott,** Kilternan, Arbuthnott, Laurencekirk AB30 1NA
	Mrs E L Hartwell, Burnigill, Burnside, Fettercairn AB30 1XY
Treasurer:	**Mrs N Lindsay,** Muirside of Thornton, Laurencekirk AB30 1EE

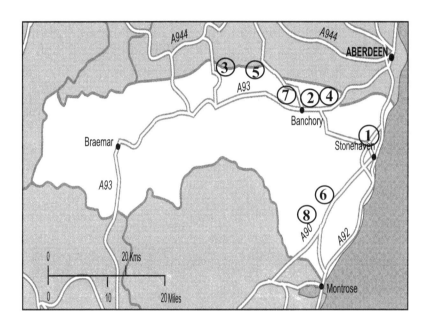

DATES OF OPENING

4 Robert Street, Stonehaven .... 1 Jul - 31 Jul by appt.   Tel. 01569 763877

Inchmarlo House Garden, Banchory	Sunday 27 May	1.30 - 4.30pm
The Burn House, Glenesk	Sunday 3 June	2 - 5pm
Crathes Castle, Banchory	Sunday 24 June	1.30 - 5pm
Findrack, Torphins	Sunday 8 July	2 - 5pm
Drum Castle, Drumoak	Sunday 15 July	12 - 5pm
Douneside House, Tarland	Sunday 22 July	2 - 5pm
Glenbervie House, Drumlithie	Sunday 5 August	2 - 5pm

1. 4 ROBERT STREET, Stonehaven AB39 2DN

(Sue & Michael Reid)

Former walled orchard filled with a wide range of climbing plants, old-fashioned and species roses. Herbacious borders, ferns and shrubs on several levels. Groups welcome.

Route: off Evan Street from Stonehaven Market Square.

Admission £2.50 Children free

1 - 31 JULY BY APPOINTMENT Tel. 01569 763877

40% to St James Church 60% net to SGS Charities

---

2. CRATHES CASTLE, Banchory AB31 5QJ

(The National Trust for Scotland)

This historic castle and its gardens are situated near Banchory and formerly the home of Sir James & Lady Burnett, whose lifelong interests found expression in the gardens and in one of the best plant collections in Britain. No less than eight colourful gardens can be found within the walled garden. Garden walks, ranger walks, forest walks.

Route: situated off A93, 3 miles east of Banchory, 15 miles west of Aberdeen.

Admission: Gardens only: £8.00 Concessions £5.00 Car park £2.00

Castle, garden, estate and use of all facilities: £10.00 Child / Concs £7.00

Family £25.00 Car park £2.00

SUNDAY 24 JUNE 1.30 - 5pm (Last entry to castle 4.45pm)

40% to The Gardens Fund of The National Trust for Scotland 60% net to SGS Charities

 (licensed restaurant) exhibitions, shop

---

3. DOUNESIDE HOUSE, Tarland AB34 4UD

(The MacRobert Trust)

Ornamental and rose gardens around a large lawn with uninterrupted views to the Deeside Hills and Grampians; large, well-stocked vegetable garden, beech walks, water gardens and new glasshouses.

Route: B9119 towards Aberdeen. Tarland 1^1/$_2$ miles.

Admission £3.00 Children & OAPs £1.00

SUNDAY 22 JULY 2 - 5pm

40% to Perennial (GRBS - Netherbyres Appeal) 60% net to SGS Charities

 (in house) local pipe band

---

4. DRUM CASTLE, Drumoak, by Banchory AB31 3EY

(The National Trust for Scotland)

In the walled garden the Trust has established a collection of old-fashioned roses which is at its peak during July. The pleasant parkland contains the 100-acre Old Wood of Drum and offers fine views and walks.

Garden walk 3pm.

Route: 10 miles west of Aberdeen and 8 miles east of Banchory on A93.

Admission Garden & Grounds only £3.00 Children £2.00

SUNDAY 15 JULY 12 - 5pm

40% to The Gardens Fund of The National Trust for Scotland 60% net to SGS Charities

---

5. FINDRACK, Torphins AB31 4LB

(Mr and Mrs Andrew Salvesen)

Carefully redesigned over the last 12 years the gardens of Findrack are set in beautiful wooded countryside and are a haven of interesting plants and unusual design features. There is a walled garden with circular lawns and deep herbaceous borders, stream garden leading to a wildlife pond, vegetable garden and woodland walk.

Route: leave Torphins on A980 to Lumphanan after $^1/_2$ mile turn off, signposted Tornaveen. Stone gateway 1 mile up on left.

Admission £3.00 Children £1.00

SUNDAY 8 JULY 2 - 5pm

40% to "The Breadmaker" Aberdeen 60% net to SGS Charities

♿ (in parts)

---

6. GLENBERVIE HOUSE, Drumlithie, Stonehaven AB39 3YB

(Mr & Mrs A Macphie)

Nucleus of present day house dates from the 15th century. Additions in 18th and 19th centuries. A traditional Scottish walled garden on a slope with roses, herbaceous and annual borders and fruit and vegetables. One wall is taken up with a fine Victorian conservatory with many varieties of pot plants and climbers on the walls, giving a dazzling display. There is also a woodland garden by a burn with primulas and ferns.

Route: Drumlithie 1 mile. Garden $1^1/_2$ miles off A90.

Admission £3.00 Children £1.00 Cars free

SUNDAY 5 AUGUST 2 - 5pm

40% to West Mearns Parish Church 60% net to SGS Charities

 baking stall

---

7. INCHMARLO HOUSE GARDEN, Banchory AB15 4AL

(Skene Enterprises (Aberdeen) Ltd)

An ever changing 5 acre woodland garden within Inchmarlo Continuing Care Retirement Community. Originally planted in the early Victorian era, featuring ancient Scots pines, Douglas firs, yews, beeches and a variety of other trees which form a dramatic background to an early summer riot of mature azaleas and rhododendrons producing a splendour of colour and scents.

Route: From Aberdeen via North Deeside Road on A93 1 mile west of Banchory, turn right at main gate to Inchmarlo House.

Admission £3.00 Children free

SUNDAY 27 MAY 1.30 - 4.30pm

40% to Alzheimer Scotland Action on Dementia 60% net to SGS Charities

♿ (limited) 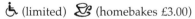 (homebakes £3.00)

---

8. THE BURN HOUSE & THE BURN GARDEN HOUSE, Glenesk DD9 7YP
(Lt. Col and Mrs G A Middlemiss for The Burn Educational Trust)
The Burn House built in 1791. Grounds of 190 acres including $2\frac{1}{2}$ mile river path by
River North Esk and a beautiful walled garden.
<u>Route:</u> 1 mile north of Edzell. Front gate situated on North side of River North Esk
bridge on B966.
<u>Admission</u> £3.00 Children under 12 free
SUNDAY 3 JUNE 2 - 5pm
40% to Special Care Baby Unit Ninewells 60% net to SGS Charities

&. ☕ (in Mansion House) also stalls and live music

LOCHABER, BADENOCH & STRATHSPEY

Joint District Organisers: **Norrie & Anna Maclaren,** Ard-Daraich, Ardgour,
Nr Fort William PH33 7AB

Treasurer: **Anna Maclaren**

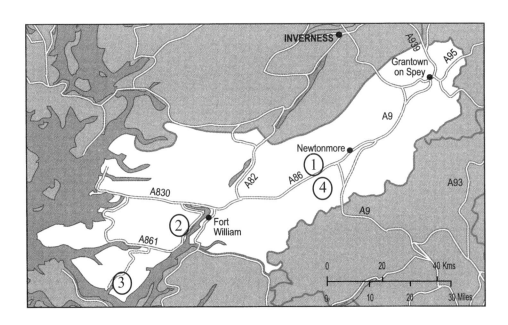

DATES OF OPENING

Ardtornish, Lochaline, Morvern .... 1 April - 31 October   10am - 6pm

Ard-Daraich, Ardgour .... Sun 20 May   12 - 5.30pm
Aberarder, Kinlochlaggan .... Sunday 27 May   2 - 5.30pm
Ardverikie, Kinlochlaggan .... Sunday 27 May   2 - 5.30pm

---

1. ABERARDER, Kinlochlaggan (Joint opening with Ardverikie)
(The Feilden Family)
Lovely garden and views over Loch Laggan.
<u>Route:</u> on A86 between Newtonmore and Spean Bridge at east end of Loch Laggan.
<u>Admission</u> combined with **ARDVERIKIE** £3.50. Children under 12 £1.00
SUNDAY 27 MAY 2 - 5.30pm
20% to Macmillan Nurses 20% to Kinlochlaggan Village Hall   60% net to SGS Charities

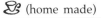 (home made)

---

2. ARD-DARAICH, Ardgour, by Fort William
(Norrie & Anna Maclaren)
Seven acre hill garden, in a spectacular setting, with many fine and uncommon rhododendrons, an interesting selection of trees and shrubs and a large collection of camellias, acers and sorbus.
<u>Route:</u> West from Fort William, across the Corran Ferry, turn left and a mile on the right further west.
<u>Admission</u> £3.50 Children under 12 £1.00
SUNDAY 20 MAY 12 - 5.30pm
20% to Highland Hospice 20% to Ardgour Memorial Hall 60% net to SGS Charities

 (in places)   (home made and light lunches) Cake stall

---

3. ARDTORNISH, by Lochaline, Morvern
(Mrs John Raven)
Garden of interesting mature conifers, rhododendrons, deciduous trees, shrubs and herbaceous set amidst magnificent scenery.
<u>Route:</u> A884. Lochaline 3 miles
<u>Entrance</u> fee charged
1 APRIL - 31 OCTOBER 10am - 6pm
Donation to Scotland's Gardens Scheme

---

4. ARDVERIKIE, Kinlochlaggan (Joint opening with Aberarder)
(Mrs P Laing & Mrs E T Smyth Osbourne)
Lovely setting on Loch Laggan with magnificent trees. Walled garden with large collection of acers, shrubs and herbaceous. Architecturally interesting house (Not open). Site of the filming of the TV series "Monarch of the Glen".
<u>Route:</u> on A86 between Newtonmore and Spean Bridge. Entrance at east end of Loch Laggan by gate lodge over bridge.
<u>Admission</u> combined with with **ABERARDER** £3.50 Children under 12 £1.00
SUNDAY 27 MAY 2 - 5.30pm
20% to Macmillan Nurses 20% to Kinlochlaggan Village Hall   60% net to SGS Charities

   (home made)

MIDLOTHIAN

District Organiser: **Mrs Richard Barron,** Laureldene, Kevock Road, Lasswade EH18 1HT

Area Organisers: **Mrs K Drummond,** Pomathorn House, Pomathorn Road, Penicuik EH26 8PJ
Mrs A M Gundlach, Fermain, 4 Upper Broomieknowe, Lasswade EH18 1LP
Mrs R Hill, 27 Biggar Road, Silverburn EH26 9LJ
Mrs E Watson, Newlandburn House, Newlandrig, Gorebridge EH23 4NS

Treasurer: **Mr A M Gundlach,** Fermain, 4 Upper Broomieknowe, Lasswade EH18 1LP

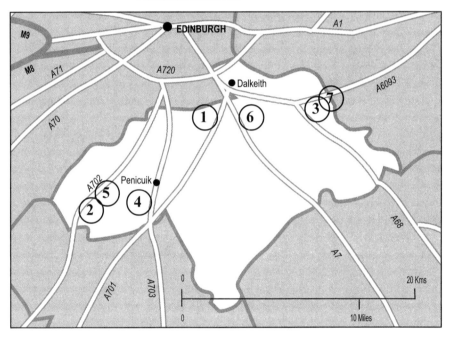

DATES OF OPENING

Newhall, Carlops .... By arrangement Tel. 01968 660206
or e.mail pak@kenmore.co.uk
The Old Sun Inn, Newbattle .... 1 May - 29 July most days by
appointment Tel. 0131 663 2648

Oxenfoord Castle, Pathhead	Sunday 15 April	2 - 5.30pm
Penicuik House, Penicuik	Sunday 27 May	2 - 5.30pm
Lasswade: 16 Kevock Road	Sat & Sun 16 & 17 June	2 - 5pm
Newhall, Carlops	Sunday 1 July	12 - 4pm
Silverburn Village Gardens, ...	Sunday 5 August	2 - 5pm

Plant Sale, Oxenfoord Mains, Pathhead. .... Saturday 13 October   9am - 2.30pm

1. LASSWADE: 16 Kevock Road EH18 1HT
(David and Stella Rankin)

A hillside garden overlooking the North Esk Valley and the ruins of Mavisbank House, with many mature trees, rhododendrons, azaleas and unusual shrubs. These are underplanted with a wide range of woodland plants and there is a pond with primula, iris and other damp loving plants. Higher up the south facing slope there are ter-races with rockeries and troughs. The garden has featured in several television programmes and magazine articles.
Route: Kevock Road lies to the south of A678 Loanhead / Lasswade Road
Admission £2.50   Children free.
SATURDAY & SUNDAY 16 & 17 JUNE 2 - 5pm
40% to St Paul's and St George's Project 21   60% net to SGS Charities

🏵 (with specialist plants)   ☕ (in Drummond Grange Nursing Home, 3 Kevock Road should be taken by 4pm - parking available)

2. NEWHALL, Carlops EH26 9LY
(John and Tricia Kennedy)
Traditional 18th century walled garden with huge herbaceous border, shrubberies, fruit and vegetables. Beautiful glen walks along the river North Esk with a wonderful selection of ferns. Large pond in the process of being planted. Many interesting perennials to view during July, some of which are for sale.
Route: on A702 Edinburgh/Biggar, a quarter of a mile after Ninemileburn and a mile before Carlops. Follow signs.
Admission £3.50 Children free
SUNDAY 1 JULY 12 - 4pm
Also by arrangement Tel. 01968 660206 or e-mail pak@kenmore.co.uk
40% William Steel Trust (RBGE) 60% net to SGS Charities

♿ (walled garden only) 🐕 🏵 ☕ (and baked potatoes) Treasure hunt

3.OXENFOORD CASTLE, near Pathhead EH22 2PF
(The Hon & Mrs Michael Dalrymple)
Extensive grounds with masses of daffodils and some early rhododendrons.
Route: A68. Opposite Gorebridge turning ³/₄ miles north of Pathhead.
Admission £2.50 Children under 12 free
SUNDAY 15 APRIL 2 - 5.30pm
40% Cranstoun Church 60% net to SGS Charities

♿ (partly) ☕ (in the castle)

4. PENICUIK HOUSE, Penicuik EH26 9LA
(Sir Robert & Lady Clerk)
Landscaped grounds with ornamental lakes, rhododendrons and azaleas. Wonderful walks.
Route: on A766 road to Carlops, Penicuik 1 mile.
Admission £2.50 Children free
SUNDAY 27 MAY 2 - 5.30pm
40% Church of St James the Less, Peniucik 60% net to SGS Charities

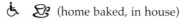 (home baked, in house)

5. SILVERBURN VILLAGE EH26
A selection of village gardens of varying size and planting style growing at 800 ft. Wonderful views and many ideas for growing plants in exposed situations.
Route: A702, 13 miles south of Edinburgh
Admission £3.00 Children free
SUNDAY 5 AUGUST 2 - 5pm
40% Silverburn Community Ltd. 60% net to SGS Charities

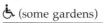 (some gardens)   (home baked)   Tombola

6. THE OLD SUN INN, Newbattle, Dalkeith EH22 3LH
(Mr & Mrs J Lochhead)
Small, half acre garden of island and raised beds containing a collection of species lilies, rock plants and some unusual bulbs - there are also two small interconnecting ponds and a conservatory.
Route: from Eskbank take B703 (Newtongrange) - garden is immediately opposite entrance to Newbattle Abbey College.
Admission £3.00 Children free
1 MAY - 29 JULY BY APPOINTMENT (most days) Tel 0131 663 2648
All to SGS Charities

  (possible)

PLANT SALE

7. SGS PLANT SALE - Joint opening East Lothian & Midlothian
held undercover at OXENFOORD MAINS, Near Pathhead EH22 2PF
Excellent selection of garden and house plants donated from private gardens.
Route: signed off A68, 4 miles south of Dalkeith.
Contact telephone number: Mrs Parker 01620 824788, Hon Michael Dalrymple 01875 320844 (office hours) or Mrs Barron 0131 663 1895.
SATURDAY 13 OCTOBER 9am- 2.30pm
40% to Cancer Research UK   60% net to SGS Charities

refreshments, home baking, fresh produce

MORAY & NAIRN

District Organiser: **Mrs J Eckersall,** Knocknagore, Knockando
Aberlour on Spey AB38 7SG

Treasurer: **Dr R Eckersall,** Knocknagore, Knockando
Aberlour on Spey AB38 7SG

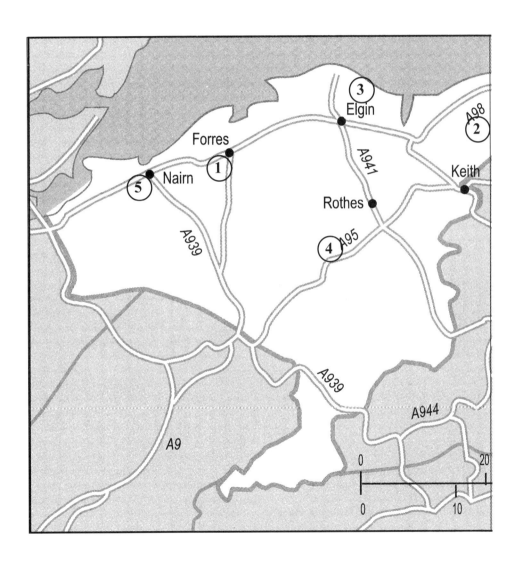

DATES OF OPENING

Knocknagore, Knockando	By appointment Fax 01340 810554	
Knocknagore, Knockando	Sunday 22 April	2 - 5pm
Woodlands, Nairn	Sunday 3 June	2 - 5pm
Carestown Steading, Deskford	Sunday 10 June	2 - 5pm
Bents Green, 10 Pilmuir Road West, Forres	Sunday 17 June	1.30 - 4.30pm
Knocknagore, Knockando	Sunday 22 July	2 - 5pm
Bents Green, 10 Pilmuir Road West, Forres	Sunday 29 July	1.30 - 4.30pm
Gordonstoun, Duffus Nr. Elgin	Sunday 9 September	2 - 4.30pm

1. BENTS GREEN, 10 Pilmuir Road West, Forres IV36 2HL

(Mrs Lorraine Dingwall)

Small town garden planted in cottage style. Formal pond, unusual plants. Interesting varieties of hosta, hardy geraniums and crocosmia.

Route: From centre of Forres take Nairn road, turn left at BP garage into Ramflat Road at end turn into Pilmuir Road then sharp left into Pilmuir Road West.

Admission Adults £2.50 Children free

SUNDAY 17 JUNE 1.30 - 4.30pm

40% Local Guiding Association 60% net to SGS Charities

SUNDAY 27 JULY 1.30 - 4.30pm

40% to Macmillan Cancer Relief 60% net to SGS Charities

2. CARESTOWN STEADING, Deskford, Buckie AB56 2TR

(Rora Paglieri)

The best compliment to Carestown garden was paid by The Garden History Society in Scotland when it described it as "Garden history in the making". The garden was started in 1990 and has received accolades from the press, TV and web (www.CarestownSteading.com). Every year a new addition is made, the latest being the epitome of the modern vegetable plot which is proving to be a great success: 4 year rotation, raised beds, seeping irrigation. Meanwhile trees and shrubs are maturing, the maze is growing, the ducks are reproducing in the three ponds and the atmosphere is as happy as ever. Not to be forgotten is the 'pearl' of the garden, the courtyard with knot beds and topiary now fully mature.

Route: East off B9018 Cullen/Keith (Cullen 3 miles, Keith 9¹/₂ miles). Follow SGS signs towards Milton and Carestown.

Admission £2.50 Children 50p

SUNDAY 10 JUNE 2 - 5pm

All takings to Scotland's Gardens Scheme

🍵 (on the barbecue area by local Guides)

3. GORDONSTOUN, Duffus, near Elgin IV30 2QZ
(The Headmaster, Gordonstoun School)
School grounds; Gordonstoun House (Georgian House of 1775/6 incorporating earlier 17th century house built for 1st Marquis of Huntly) and school chapel - both open. Unique circle of former farm buildings known as the Round Square.
Route: entrance off B9012, 4 miles from Elgin at Duffus Village.
Admission £2.50 Children £1.00
SUNDAY 9 SEPTEMBER 2 - 4.30pm
All takings to Scotland's Gardens Scheme

4. KNOCKNAGORE, Knockando
(Dr and Mrs Eckersall)
A series of gardens created from rough pasture and moorland since 1995. Comprising trees, herbaceous beds, rockery, courtyard garden and "Sittie Ooterie". Vegetable plot and two ponds, all surrounded by stunning views.
Route: entrance from 'Cottage Road' which connects the B9102 Archiestown to Knockando Road with the Knockando to Dallas Road.
Admission Adults £2.50 Children 50p
SUNDAY 22 APRIL 2 - 5pm
An opening in April to give the opportunity to see the spring flowers featuring the daffodils..
SUNDAY 22 JULY 2 - 5pm
Open other times by prior appointment Fax no. 01340 810554
40% to Dialysis Unit, Dr. Gray's Hospital, Elgin 60% net to SGS Charities

5. WOODLANDS, Nairn IV12 5NG NEW
(Mrs A MacLennan)
Mature woodland garden, created from scrubland in 1990, covering approx. 1 acre, incorporating many choice and specimen trees and shrubs. Includes several water features, waterfalls and rockeries with a natural stream flowing through. There are various borders and beds with hostas, grasses and waterside plants.
Route: leave Nairn on A96 heading west towards Inverness. Approx ³/₄ mile from Nairn Town Centre turn left onto Tradespark Road; "Woodlands" is 50 yards along on the right.
Admission Adults £2.50 Children 50p
SUNDAY 3 JUNE 2 - 5pm - Teas & Plant Stall
40% to Chest, Heart & Stroke 60% net to SGS Charities

PERTH & KINROSS

District Organisers: **The Hon Mrs Ranald Noel-Paton**, Pitcurran House, Abernethy PH2 9LH
Mrs D J W Anstice, Broomhill, Abernethy PH2 9LQ

Area Organisers: **Mrs C Dunphie,** Wester Cloquhat, Bridge of Cally PH10 7JP
Miss L Heriot Maitland, Keepers Cottage, Hill of Errol PH2 7TQ
Mrs M Innes, Kilspindie Manse, Kilspindie PH2 7RX
Lady Livesay, Bute Cottage, Academy Road, Crieff PH7 4AT
Mrs P Mackenzie, Baledmund House, Pitlochry PH16 5RA
Mrs D Nichol, Rossie House, Forgandenny PH2 9EH
Miss Judy Norwell, 20 Pitcullen Terrace, Perth PH2 7EQ
Mrs Athel Price, Bolfracks, Aberfeldy PH15 2EX
Miss Bumble Ogilvy Wedderburn, Garden Cottage, Lude, Blair Atholl, PH18 5TR

Treasurer: **Mr Cosmo Fairbairn**, Alleybank, Bridge of Earn, Perth PH2 9EZ

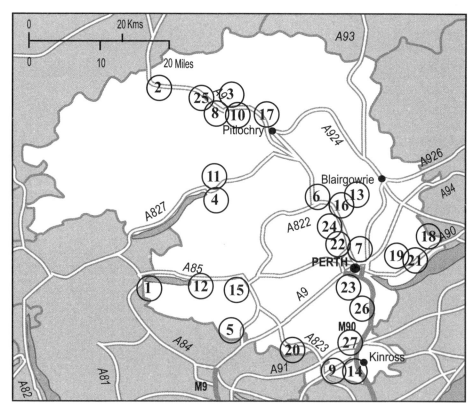

DATES OF OPENING

Ardvorlich, Lochearnhead	6 May to 3 June	All day
Bolfracks, Aberfeldy	1 April - 31October	10am - 6pm
Braco Castle, Braco	1 February - 31 October	10am - 5pm
Cluniemore, Pitlochry	May - 1 Oct. by Appt.	01796 472006
Cluny House, Aberfeldy	1 March - 31 October	10am - 6pm
Dowhill, Cleish	April & June Thursday's	1pm - 4pm
Drummond Castle Gardens, Crieff	May - October Daily	2pm - 6pm
Easter Meikle Fardle, Meikleour	May - Mid Aug. by Appt.	01738 710330
Glendoick, by Perth	9 April - 8 June Mon - Fri	10pm - 4pm
Rossie House, Forgandenny	March - 31 Oct. by Appt.	01738 812265
Scone Palace, Perth	1 April - 31 October	9.30 - 5pm
Strathgarry House, Killiecrankie	June, July, Aug. by Appt.	01796 481466
The Bank House, Glenfarg	Mid May-31 Aug. groups by Appt.	01577 830275
Wester Dalqueich, Carnbo	May - 31 Aug. by Appt.	01577 840229

Megginch Castle. Errol	Sunday 15 April	2 - 5pm
Glendoick, by Perth	Sunday 6 May	2 - 5pm
Branklyn, Perth	Sunday 6 May	10am - 5pm
Glendoick, by Perth	Sunday 20 May	2 - 5pm
Fingask Castle, Rait	Sunday 27 May	2 - 5.30pm
Delvine, Spittalfield	Sunday 3 June	2 - 6pm
Comrie Village Gardens, Comrie	Sunday 10 June	1 - 5.30pm
Explorers, Pitlochry	Sunday 17 June	11am - 5pm
Bradystone House, Murthly	Sunday 17 June	11am - 4pm
Blair Castle Gardens, Blair Atholl	Sunday 24 June	9.30am - 5.30pm
Cleish Gardens, Cleish	Sunday 24 June	2 - 5pm
Carig Dhubh, Bonskeid	Sunday 1 July	11am - 5pm
Strathgarry House, Killiecrankie	Sunday 1 July	11am - 5pm
Comrie Village Gardens, Comrie	Sunday 8 July	1 - 5.30pm
Auchleeks House, Trinafour	Sunday 15 July	2 - 6pm
Hollytree Lodge, Pool o'Muckhart	Sunday 29 July	2 - 5pm
Drummond Castle Gardens, Crieff	Sunday 5 August	2 - 6pm
Comrie Village Gardens, Comrie	Sunday 12 August	1 - 5.30pm
Mount Tabor House, Perth	Sunday 12 August	2 - 5.30pm

1. ARDVORLICH, Lochearnhead FK19 8QE

(Mr & Mrs Sandy Stewart)

Beautiful glen with rhododendrons (species and many hybrids) grown in wild conditions amid oaks and birches. Quite steep in places. Gum boots advisable when wet.

<u>Route:</u> on South Lochearn Road 3 miles from Lochearnhead, 4^1/$_2$ miles from St Fillans.

<u>Admission</u> £3.00   Children under 12 free

6 MAY to 3 JUNE ALL DAY

40% to The Gurkha Welfare Trust 60% net to SGS Charities

2. AUCHLEEKS HOUSE, Calvine PH18 5UF
(Mr & Mrs Angus MacDonald)
Auchleeks is a classical Georgian house with a large herbaceous walled garden in a beautiful glen setting, surrounded by hills and mature trees.
Route: North of Blair Atholl turn off A9 at Calvine. B847 towards Kinloch Rannoch, 5 miles on right.
Admission £3.00 Children free
SUNDAY 15 JULY 2 - 6pm
40% to Struan Primary School 60% net to SGS Charities

---

3. BLAIR CASTLE GARDENS, Blair Atholl PH18 5TL
(Blair Charitable Trust)
Blair Castle stands as the focal point in a designed landscape of some 2,500 acres within a large and traditional estate. Hercules Garden is a walled enclosure of about 9 acres recently restored to its original 18th Century form with landscaped ponds, plantings, fruit trees, vegetables, herbaceous gardens and landscape features. Diana's Grove is a magnificent stand of tall trees including grand fir, douglas fir, larch and wellingtonia in just two acres.
Route: off A9, follow signs to Blair Castle, Blair Atholl.
Admission Adults/OAP's £2.50 Families £5.70 Children £1.30 Group Rates
SUNDAY 24 JUNE 9.30 - 5.30pm
Donation to Scotland's Gardens Scheme

♿ (partly)

---

4. BOLFRACKS, Aberfeldy PH15 2EX
(The Douglas Hutchison Trust)
3 acre north facing garden with wonderful views overlooking the Tay valley. Burn garden with rhododendrons, azaleas, primulas, meconopsis, etc. in woodland setting. Walled garden with shrubs, herbaceous borders, old fashioned roses and clematis. Great selection of bulbs in the spring and good autumn colour with sorbus, gentians and cyclamen. Slippery paths and bridges in wet weather.
Route: 2 miles west of Aberfeldy on A827. White gates and Lodge on left.
Admission £3.00 Children under 16 free
1 APRIL - 31 OCTOBER 10am - 6pm
Donation to Scotland's Gardens Scheme

✿ (limited)

Parties, including lunch and teas, available by prior arrangement, please telephone 01887 820344.

110

5. BRACO CASTLE, Braco FK15 9LA
(Mr & Mrs M van Ballegooijen)
A 19th Century landscaped garden comprising woodland and meadow walks with a fine show of spring flowering bulbs, many mature specimen trees and shrubs, with considerable new planting. The partly walled garden is approached on a rhododendron and tree-lined path and features an ornamentsl pond, extensive hedging and lawns with shrub and herbaceous borders. The planting is enhanced by spectacular views over the castle park to the Ochils. Good autumn colour.
Route: 1 to 1¹/₂ mile drive from gates at north end of Braco Village, just west of bridge on A822.
Admission £3.00 Children free
1 FEBRUARY - 31 OCTOBER EVERY DAY 10 - 5pm
40% to The Woodland Trust 60% net to SGS Charities
♿ (partly)

---

6. BRADYSTONE HOUSE, Murthly PH1 4EW
(Mr & Mrs James Lumsden)
True cottage courtyard garden converted eleven years ago from derelict farm steadings. Ponds, free roaming ducks and hens and many interesting shrubs and ornamental trees.
Route: from south/north follow A9 to Bankfoot, then sign to Murthly. At crossroads in Murthly take private road to Bradystone.
Admission £3.00
SUNDAY 17 JUNE 11am - 4pm
40% to Caputh and Clunie Church 60% net to SGS Charities
♿ (partly) 🌸 (Soup and filled rolls, etc.)

---

7. BRANKLYN, Perth PH2 7BB
(The National Trust for Scotland)
This attractive little garden in Perth was once described as "the finest two acres of private garden in the country". It contains an outstanding collection of plants, particularly rhododendrons, alpine, herbaceous and peat-loving plants, which attract gardeners and botanists from all over the world.
Route: on A85 Perth/Dundee road.
Admission £5.00 Concessions £4.00 Family £14.00
SUNDAY 6 MAY 10am - 5pm
40% to The Gardens Fund of The National Trust for Scotland 60% net to SGS Charities
♿ (parking at gate)

---

8. CARIG DHUBH, Bonskeid PH16 5NP NEW
(Mr & Mrs Niall Graham-Campbell)
The garden is comprised of mixed shrubs and herbaceous plants with mecanopsis and primulas. It extends to about one acre on the side of a hill with some steep paths and uneven ground. The soil is sand overlying rock - some of which projects through the surface. Beautiful surrounding country and hill views.
Route: take old A9 between Pitlochry and Killiecrankie, midway turn west on the Tummel Bridge Road B8019, ³/₄ mile on North of the road.
Admission £3.00 Children under 16 free
SUNDAY 1 JULY 11am - 5pm - together with STRATHGARRY HOUSE, Killiecrankie
40% to Tenandry Kirk 60% net to SGS Charities
 🌸 (some)

---

9. CLEISH GARDENS, Cleish
Cleish House KY13 0LR (Mr & Mrs D Erskine)
Boreland House KY13 0LN(Mr & Mrs N Kilpatrick)
Old School House KY13 7LR (Mr & Mrs F Whalley)
Kirkdale KY13 0LR (Mr & Mrs R Kitchin)
Four charming Village Gardens, of which three are mature and one is 12 years old and under development. Another attraction is the Village Enhancement Scheme Walk down to and along Gairney Burn.
Route: J5 off M90, take B9097 towards Crook of Devon, Cleish 2^1/$_2$ miles.
Admission £3.50 Children free
SUNDAY 24 JUNE 2 - 5pm
40% to Kinross-shire Volunteer Group and Rural Outreach Scheme 60% net to SGS Charities

 (at Boreland House) (in Village Hall)

---

10. CLUNIEMORE, Pitlochry PH16 5NE
(Major Sir David & Lady Butter)
Mature garden in a beautiful setting surrounded by hills. Rock and water gardens, lawns, herbaceous and annual border. Roses, shrubs and a short (signed) woodland walk above the garden. Greenhouses.
Route: on A9 Pitlochry bypass.
Admission £3.00 Children under 16 free
1 MAY - 1 OCTOBER by appointment please telephone 01796 472006
40% to The Pushkin Prizes in Scotland 60% net to SGS Charities

---

11. CLUNY HOUSE, Aberfeldy PH15 2JT
(Mr J & Mrs W Mattingley)
A wonderful, wild woodland garden overlooking the scenic Strathtay valley. Experience the grandeur of one of Britain's widest trees, the complex leaf variation of the Japanese maple, the beauty of the American trillium or the diversity of Asiatic primulas. A treasure not to be missed.
Route: 3^1/$_2$ miles from Aberfeldy on Weem to Strathtay Road.
Admission £3.50   Children under 16 free
1 MARCH - 31 OCTOBER 10am - 6pm
Donation to Scotland's Gardens Scheme

---

12. COMRIE VILLAGE GARDENS, Comrie PH6 2PF **NEW**
(Comrie Gardeners)
Comrie is an award winning Britain in Bloom Village straddling the River Earn with stunning views to the surrounding hills. A number of gardens will be open including a plantswoman's with some rare flowers and vegetables, a riverside haven for wildlife and several which have colourful displays of annuals and containers.
Route: from A85 turn into Bridle Street (between RBoS and White Church), follow road past fire station, first left. Tickets and map from Pat Onions, 21 Tay Avenue.
Admission £3.50 Children free
SUNDAYS 10 JUNE, 8 JULY, 12 AUGUST 1 - 5.30pm
20% to Irish Setters Rescue 20% Comrie in Colour 60% net to SGS Charities

 (partly)

13. DELVINE, Spittalfield PH1 4LD
(Mr & Mrs David Gemmell)
The gardens at Delvine are situated on Inchtuthill (the island that floods), an old
Roman Legionary fortress abandoned 85AD. In a wild and secluded setting a new
arboretum and water project is taking shape below the existing gardens with
wonderful views. The area is surrounded by particularly fine and very old trees.
Route: on A984, 7 miles east of Dunkeld, 4 miles south west of Blairgowrie.
Admission £3.00 Children 50p
SUNDAY 3 JUNE 2 - 6pm
40% to Maggie's Centre 60% net to SGS Charities

♿ (only near house) ☕

---

14. DOWHILL, Cleish KY4 0HZ
(Mr & Mrs Colin Maitland Dougall)
A garden of interst to those who like water and ponds, set off by a background of
wonderful mature trees. The ponds, rhododendrons, primulas and blue poppies blend
into the natural landscape. Woodland walks to the ruins of Dowhill Castle.
Route: ³/₄ mile off M90, exit 5, towards Crook of Devon.
Admission £3.00
APRIL and JUNE THURSDAYS 1pm - 4pm
40% to Children's Hospice, Kinross 60% net to SGS charities

♿ (partly) ☕ (only if requested)

---

15. DRUMMOND CASTLE GARDENS, Crieff PH5 2AA
(Grimsthorpe & Drummond Castle Trust Ltd)
The Gardens of Drummond Castle were originally laid out in 1630 by John
Drummond, 2nd Earl of Perth. In 1830 the parterre was changed to an Italian style.
One of the most interesting features is the multi-faceted sundial designed by John
Mylne, Master Mason to Charles I. The formal garden is said to be one of the finest
in Europe and is the largest of its type in Scotland.
Route: entrance 2 miles south of Crieff on Muthill road (A822).
Admission £3.00 OAPs £2.00 Children £1.00
SUNDAY 5 AUGUST 1 - 5pm
MAY - OCTOBER DAILY 2 - 6pm (last entrance 5pm)
40% to British Limbless Ex-Servicemen's Association 60% net to SGS Charities

♿ ☕ raffle, entertainments and stalls

---

16. EASTER MEIKLE FARDLE, Meikleour PH2 6EF
(Rear Admiral and Mrs John Mackenzie)
A delightful 2 acre garden created in the last 11 years. Herbaceous borders backed by soft
sandstone or beech hedges - the latter only 6 years old. Small enclosed garden with raised
beds and newly formed water and bog garden. Walks through maturing woodland. This
garden gives an insight into what is achievable in a short space of time.
Route: take A984 Dunkeld to Coupar Angus 1¹/₂ miles, from Spittalfield towards
Meikleour, third house on left after turning to Lethendy.
Admission £3.00 Children free
1 MAY - MID AUGUST BY APPOINTMENT 2 - 5pm TEL: 01738 710330
40% to Perth Sea Cadets 60% net to SGS Charities

♿ (mostly) ❁ (small) ☕ (and light refreshments by arrangement)

---

17. EXPLORERS, The Scottish Plant Hunters Garden, Pitlochry PH16 5DR

A wonderful new garden overlooking the River Tummel, planted with a mixture of species and cultivars to represent The Scottish Plant Collectors.
Route: A9 to Pitlochry town, follow signs to Pitlochry Festival Theatre.
Admission £3.00 Children £1.00
SUNDAY 17 JUNE 10am - 5pm
40% to Acting for Others   60% net to SGS Charities

  (at Theatre)

---

18. FINGASK CASTLE, Rait PH2 7SA

(Mr & Mrs Andrew Murray Threipland)
17th Century garden with largest collection of topiary in Scotland. Woodland walks, covered bridges, lakes, bamboos etc.
Route: Halfway between Perth and Dundee (A90), follow signs to Rait.
Admission £3.00 Children free
SUNDAY 27 MAY 2 - 5.30pm
20% to Fingask Follies 20% to Refugee Council 60% net to SGS Charities

(limited)

---

19. GLENDOICK, by Perth PH2 7NS

(Peter, Patricia, Kenneth & Jane Cox)
Glendoick was recently included in the 'Independent on Sunday's' exclusive survey of Europe's top 50 gardens and boasts a unique collection of plants collected by 3 generations of Coxes from their plant-hunting expeditions to China and the Himalayas. Fine collection of rhododendrons, azaleas, primula, meconopsis, kalmia and sorbus in the enchanting woodland garden with naturalised wild flowers. Extensive peat garden, nursery and hybrid trial garden.
Route: follow signs to Glendoick Garden Centre off A90 Perth - Dundee road.
Admission £3.00 School children free
SUNDAYS 6 & 20 MAY 2 - 5pm
Donation to Scotland's Gardens Scheme and WWF
Also 9 April - 8 June Monday - Friday 10am - 4pm

 (only garden by house) (meals and snacks available at Glendoick Garden Centre)

---

20. HOLLYTREE LODGE, Pool O'Muckart FK14 7JW

(Maureen & David Miller)
1$^1/_2$ acre garden containing many rare and unusual trees, shrubs and herbaceous plants. There are woodland areas containing a collection of rhododendron species, a peat border, fernery, a moorland bed and various shrub plantings. More formal areas include several herbaceous borders, some themed by colour and a bed devoted entirely to ornamental grasses. Water features and a rock garden. A Japanese courtyard garden, semi-formal potager and terrace with tender pot plants set off the house (not open).
Route: off A91 down lane opposite the 'Inn at Muckhart'. Park on the main road.
Admission £3.00 Children free.
SUNDAY 29 JULY 2 - 5pm
40% to Thrive 60% net to SGS Charities

(partly) (in the Village Hall)

21. MEGGINCH CASTLE, Errol PH2 7SW

(Captain Humphrey Drummond of Megginch & Mr Giles & Hon. Mrs Herdman)
15th century turreted castle (not open) with Gothic courtyard and pagoda dovecote. 1,000 year old yews and topiary. Astrological garden. Daffodils and rhododendrons. Water garden.
Route: approach from Dundee only, directly off A90, on south side of carriageway, ¹/₂ mile on left after Errol flyover, between lodge gatehouses. (7 miles from Perth, 8 from Dundee).
Admission £3.00 Children free
SUNDAY 15 APRIL 2 - 5pm
40% to All Saints Church, Glencarse   60% net to SGS Charities

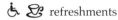 refreshments

22. MOUNT TABOR HOUSE, Mount Tabor Road, Perth PH2 7DE

(Mr & Mrs John McEwan)
Mature terraced town garden originally laid out in the late 19th Century surrounded by trees and herbaceous borders. Water feature.
Route: from Dundee Road in Perth at Isle of Skye Hotel, turn right into Manse Road, over mini-roundabout and into Mount Tabor Road.
Admission £3.00
SUNDAY 12 AUGUST 2 - 5.30pm
20% to Mercy Ships 20 % Kinnoull Parish Church Restoration Fund 60% net to SGS Charities

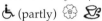 (partly)

23. ROSSIE HOUSE, Forgandenny PH2 9EH

This mature woodland garden, with undulating terrain including a water garden and a walled garden, provides year round interest. In early spring snowdrops and aconites are chased on by bluebells and other woodland plants beneath rhododendron, specimen trees, cornuses and a large davidia involucrata. Other interesting trees to see in July and August are the fragrant magnolia hypoluca, a lovely stewartia followed by lacecap hydrangeas and intense autumn colour. Sculptures by David Annand and Nigel Ross. The walled garden with Victorian greenhouse and old fashioned roses also holds rare breeds of sheep.
Admission £3.00 Children free
1 MARCH TO 31 OCTOBER BY APPOINTMENT Tel. 01738 812265
40% to Sandpiper Trust 60% net to SGS Charities

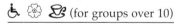 (for groups over 10)

24. SCONE PALACE, Perth PH2 6BE

(The Earl & Countess of Mansfield)
Extensive and well laid out grounds and a magnificent pinetum dating from 1848; there is a Douglas fir raised from the original seed sent from America in 1824. The woodland garden has attractive walks amongst the rhododendrons and azaleas and leads into the Monks' Playgreen and Friar's Den of the former Abbey of Scone.
Route: A93. Perth 2 miles.
Admission (grounds only) £4.00 Students & OAP's £3.65 Children £2.75
1 APRIL - 31 OCTOBER 9.30am - 5.30pm (last entry 5pm)
Donation to Scotland's Gardens Scheme

Murray Star beech maze

25. STRATHGARRY HOUSE, Killiecrankie PH16 5LJ

(Mr & Mrs S Thewes)

Early 19th Century walled garden laid out in a cruciform and set in beautiful surroundings. A large collection of apple trees, some of which are presently unknown, others are rare, old Scottish varieties and are underplanted with large herbaceous borders. Raised vegetable garden and small courtyard garden also with raised borders.

Route: between Pitlochry-Blair Atholl, off the old A9 at Killiecrankie.

Admission £3.00   Children under 16 free

SUNDAY 1 JULY 11am - 5pm together with CARIG DHUBH, Bonskeid

Also June, July & August groups by appointment Tel. 01796 481466

40% to Kilmaveonaig Church   60% net to SGS Charities

 (home made soup, rolls and gingerbread)

26. THE BANK HOUSE, Glenfarg PH2 9NZ

(Mr & Mrs C B Lascelles)

A large garden (for the centre of a village) in two parts. Behind the house a tunnel of apple trees leads from a stone-paved area into the main garden of shrubs and unusual herbaceous plants. Pond, fountains, sculpture; raised-bed vegetable system, organic methods throughout; advanced compost-making equipment. Across the road, water cascades down steps to a further garden with a wildlife pond and ornamental trees. Also a wildflower meadow and a winter bed at far end.

Route: Exit 8 or 9 from M90. Situated 50 yds. down side road by Glenfarg Hotel.

Admission £5.00

MID MAY - 31 AUGUST BY APPOINTMENT TEL. 01577 830275

40% to The Phoenix Prison Trust   60% net to SGS Charities

 (mostly)

27. WESTER DALQUEICH, Carnbo KY13 7NU

(Mr & Mrs D S Roulston)

A series of interconnected gardens in three and a half acres by the Ochil Hills. A wide range of herbaceous, rock plants, shrubs and tree planting.

Route: Leave A91 at Carnbo Village Hall, West of Milnathort and travel north for $^{1}/_{2}$ mile.

Admission £3.00

1 MAY - 31 AUGUST BY APPOINTMENT TEL. 01577 840229

40% to Chest, Heart & Stroke, Scotland   60% net to SGS Charities

♿ (partly) ☕ (on request)

Our website, www.gardensofscotland.org, provides information on Scotland's Gardens Scheme and the gardens that open for us.

The site will be re-designed in the course of 2007

RENFREW & INVERCLYDE

Joint District Organisers:	**Mrs J R Hutton,** Auchenclava, Finlaystone, Langbank PA14 6TJ
	Mrs Daphne Ogg, Nittingshill, Kilmacolm PA13 4SG
Area Organisers:	**Lady Denholm,** Newton of Bell Trees, Lochwinnoch PA12 4JL
	Mrs Rosemary Leslie, High Mathernock Farm, Auchentiber Road, Kilmalcolm.
	Mr J A Wardrop DL, St Kevins, Victoria Road, Paisley PA2 9PT
PR -	**Mrs G West,** Woodlands, 2 Birchwood Road, Uplawmoor, G78 4DG
Treasurer:	**Mrs Jean Gillan,** Bogriggs Cottage, Carlung, West Kilbride KA23 9PS

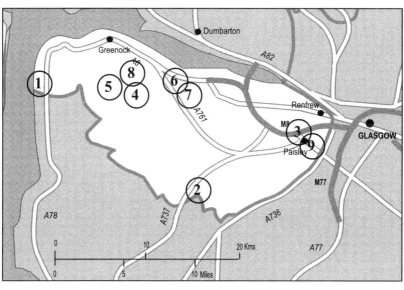

DATES OF OPENING

Ardgowan, Inverkip	Sunday 18 February	2 - 5pm
Auchengrange and Lochside, Lochwinnoch	Sunday 25 February	2 - 5pm
Finlaystone, Langbank	Sunday 1 April	2 - 5pm
Kilmacolm Gardens,	Sunday 13 May	2 - 5pm
Carruth, Bridge of Weir	Sunday 3 June	2 - 5pm
Bridge of Weir Gardens,	Sunday 17 June	2 - 5pm
Houston Gardens.	Sunday 26 August	2 - 5pm

(Please note: Entry in Monthly Calendar List on page 21 is incorrect)

Sma' Shot Cottages Heritage Centre, Paisley	Saturday 30 June	2 - 5pm
Barshaw Park, Paisley	Sunday 19 August	2 - 5pm
Carruth Plant Sale, Bridge of Weir	Sunday 3 June	2 - 5pm
Finlaystone Plant Sale, Langbank	Sunday 2 September	11.30am - 4pm

117

1. ARDGOWAN, Inverkip PA16 0DW

(Lady Shaw Stewart)

Woodland walks carpeted with snowdrops. (Strong waterproof footwear advised).

Route: Inverkip 1¹/₂ miles. Glasgow/Largs buses to and from Inverkip Village

Admission £2.00 Children under 10 free

SUNDAY 18 FEBRUARY 2 - 5pm

40% to Ardgowan Hospice 60% net to SGS Charities

♿ (not advisable if wet) ❀ (and snowdrops) ☕ (in house) Tombola, home produce

---

2. AUCHENGRANGE & LOCHSIDE, Lochwinnoch PA12 4JS

Auchengrange (John & Jan Davies) **Lochside** (Keith & Kate Lough)

Two mature woodland gardens carpeted with snowdrops.

Route: Auchengrange - from A737 at Lochwinnoch/Largs roundabout at Iron Art Forge, head south up Auchengrange Hill, short drive to entrance gate.

Lochside A737 200 yards east of Lochwinnoch/Largs roundabout. White railings on north side of road. Also direct pedestrian access via RSPB Lochwinnoch Reserve.

Admission £3.00 (includes both gardens) Children free

SUNDAY 25 FEBRUARY 2 - 5pm

40% to Alzheimers Scotland 60% net to SGS Charities

♿ ❀ (at Lochside) ☕ (at Auchengrange)

---

3. BARSHAW PARK - Walled Garden, Paisley PA1 1UG

(Environmental Services Department, Renfrewshire Council)

Walled garden displaying a varied selection of plants, some of which are suitable for the blind to smell and feel. These would include a colourful layout of summer bedding plants, herbaceous borders, mixed shrub borders and rose beds.

Route: from Paisley town centre along the Glasgow road (A737) pass Barshaw Park and take first left into Oldhall Road & then first left again into walled garden car park. Pedestrian visitors can also approach from Barshaw Park by mid gate in Glasgow Road

Admission by donation

SUNDAY 19 AUGUST 2 - 5pm

40% to Erskine Hospital 60% net to SGS Charities

♿ (gravel paths) ❀ ☕ (home-made)

GARDENING TIP

Cover the hole of a clay pot with a spent tea bag to avoid blocking the hole.

4. BRIDGE OF WEIR GARDENS
Airlie, Prieston Road PA11 3AN(Mrs Helen Crichton)
Large garden with fine herbaceous borders in immaculate order.
Craigend, Montrose Terrace PA11 3DH (Anthony and Randy Rush)
Thoughtfully laid out garden. Sculptures. Attractive planting. Pond.
Hazelwood, Hazelwood Road PA11 3DB (Dr Alison Moss) NEW
1^1/$_2$ acres, established 1870. Emphasis on unusual shrubs and trees. Wildlife garden. NB some steep paths requiring agility.
Hillcrest, Bonar Crescent PA11 3EH (Donald & Nan Blair) NEW
Small garden shared with insects and birds. Raised beds for growing vegetables in old age.
<u>Route:</u> at east end of village, turn off from A761 at Clydesdale Bank and right into Prieston Road. Thereafter well signed.
<u>Admission</u> £3.00 to cover all 4 gardens at which maps will be available
SUNDAY 17 JUNE 2 - 5pm
40% to Multiple Sclerosis   60% net to SGS Charities

 (at Airlie)    (at Craigend)

---

5. CARRUTH, Bridge of Weir PA11 3SG
(Mr & Mrs Charles Maclean)
Large Plant Sale including a wide selection of herbaceous, herbs, shrubs etc. Over 20 acres of long established rhododendrons, woodland and lawn gardens in lovely landscaped setting.Young arboretum.
<u>Route:</u> access from B786 Kilmacolm/Lochwinnoch road or from Bridge of Weir via Torr Road.
<u>Admission</u> £3.00
SUNDAY 3 JUNE 2 - 5pm
40% to Marié Curie Cancer Care 60% net to SGS Charities

 (home made)

---

6. FINLAYSTONE, Langbank PA14 6TJ
(Mr & Mrs Arthur MacMillan)
Historic connection with John Knox and Robert Burns. Richly varied gardens with unusual plants overlooking the Clyde. A profusion of daffodils and early rhododendrons. Waterfalls and pond. Woodland walks with imaginative play and picnic areas.
<u>Route:</u> on A8 west of Langbank, 10 minutes by car west of Glasgow Airport.
<u>Admission</u> £3.50 Children (under 4 free) & OAPs £2.50
SUNDAY 1 APRIL 2 - 5pm
40% to The Lilias Graham Trust 60% net to SGS Charities

♿ (significant)   (in the Celtic Tree in the walled garden)   Doll museum, Ranger service, "Eye-opener" centre with shop
Website: www.finlaystone.co.uk

---

7. HOUSTON GARDENS
Five cottage gardens in conservation village of Houston within reasonable walking distance of each other.

a) Old Police House, Main Street PA6 7EL (John & June Wilson) [NEW]
Cottage garden containing shrubs and bedding plants

b) Rosemount Cottage, Main Street PA6 7EL (Adam & Kathryn McCartney) [NEW]
Cottage garden, shrubs, herbaceous containers, bedding annuals

c) Strathyre, Main Street PA6 7EL (Victor Holmes) [NEW]
Cottage garden, flower beds with vegetable plot.

d) Owersby, 34 Manse Crescent PA6 7JN (George & Marjory Spark) [NEW]
Bedding borders and patio plant containers

e) Kilfillan, Houston Road PA6 7BA (Graeme & Shona Crawford) [NEW]
On the outskirts of the village of Houston the garden has been planted out over the past 10 years and includes a good variety of conifers, shrubs, herbaceous and rock plants. The rear garden includes a pond with goldfish.

<u>Route:</u> approach village by B790 or B789. Gardens a, b & c and church hall in village centre, on B789; d and e nearby and well signposted.

<u>Admission</u> £3.00 (includes entry to all gardens) Children under 10 free

SUNDAY 26 AUGUST 2 - 5pm

40% Accord Hospice 60% net to SGS Charities
Teas in aid of Accord Hospice Plant sales for SGS Charities

 ♿ ✿ (by Church Hall) ☕ (at Houston and Killellan Church Hall, Main Street)

8. KILMACOLM GARDENS PA13
Cloak, Cloak Road, by Kilmacolm (Victoria Murday and Annabel & Gareth Inman)
Set in $3^1/_2$ acres beside Auchendores Reservoir. Herbaceous borders, woodlands, kitchen gardens. Rennie MacIntosh feature.

<u>Route:</u> to avoid congestion, traffic should approach Cloak Road off A761 (Kilmacolm to Port Glasgow road) and depart continuing on Cloak Road to Finlaystone Road, then right to Kilmacolm.

Nether Knockbuckle, Hazelmere Road (John & Sheila Hamilton) [NEW]
Large informal garden with woodland and bluebells, beside River Gryfe. Interesting sculptures.

<u>Route:</u> from Kilmacolm Cross along Lochwinnoch Road. Turn right into Knockbuckle Road, left into Florence Drive. Signed thereafter. A minibus will circulate between the two venues and the church hall. First departure St Fillans Church Hall 1.45pm (£2.00 charge)

<u>Admission</u> £3.00

SUNDAY 13 MAY 2 - 5pm

20% UNICEF 20% Cancer Research 60% net to SGS Charities

✿ (at St Fillans Church Hall, Moss Road) ☕ (at St Fillans Church Hall, Moss Road)

9. SMA' SHOT COTTAGES HERITAGE CENTRE, 11 /17 George Place PaisleyPA1 2HZ
(Old Paisley Society)
Small enclosed courtyard garden. Enjoy the 19th Century weaver's garden designed to celebrate the 21st anniversary of Sma' Shot Cottages. All plants are true to the period. Assistance in the creation of the garden was provided by the Beechgrove gardeners. Visitors may also see the rare "Paisley Gem" (Dianthus) and the new "Viola Sma' Shot Cottages" bred by local gardener, Hugh Boyd.
Route: off New Street in Paisley Town Centre.
Admission £2.00   Children free
SATURDAY 30 JUNE 2 - 5pm
40% Old Paisley Society 60% net to SGS Charities

  (home baked in Heritage Centre) Heritage Centre Tours (free)   Gift shop

PLANT SALES

(5) CARRUTH, Bridge of Weir PA11 3SG
(Mr & Mrs Charles Maclean)
A plant sale in conjunction with garden opening (see also garden no. 5)
Route: access from B786 Kilmacolm/Lochwinnoch road or from Bridge of Weir via Torr Road.
Admission £3.00
SUNDAY 3 JUNE 2 - 5pm
40% to Marié Curie Cancer Care 60% net to SGS Charities

  (home made)

(6) FINLAYSTONE, Langbank PA14 6TJ
(Mr & Mrs Arthur MacMillan)
An opportunity to purchase plants at the end of season clearance sale. Finlaystone gardens and woodlands will be open as usual on this day (see also garden no. 6).
Route: on A8 west of Langbank, 10 minutes by car west of Glasgow Airport.
SUNDAY 2 SEPTEMBER SGS SPECIAL PLANT SALE 11.30am - 4pm
40% of plant sales to Promoting Equality in African Schools 60% net to SGS Charities

Website: www.finlaystone.co.uk

ROSS, CROMARTY, SKYE & INVERNESS

District Organiser: **Lady Lister-Kaye,** House of Aigas, Beauly IV4 7AD

Treasurer: **Mrs Shelia Kerr,** Lilac Cottage, Struy, by Beauly IV4 7JU

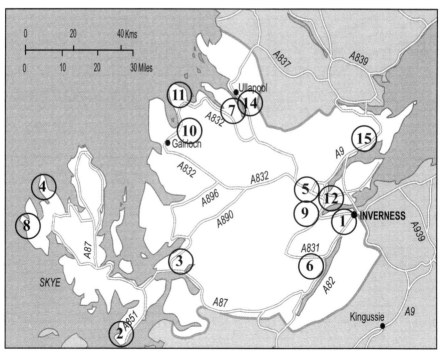

DATES OF OPENING

Abriachan, Loch Ness Side	February - November	9am - dusk
An Acarsaid, Ord, Isle of Skye	April - October	10am - 5.30pm
Attadale, Strathcarron	1 Apr - 31 Oct (Closed Sun)	10am - 5.30pm
Balmeanach House, Struan	Wed & Sat 30 Apr - mid Oct	11am - 4.30pm
Coiltie Garden, Divach, Drumnadrochit	20 June - 20 July daily	Noon - 7pm
Dunvegan Castle, Isle of Skye	Mid Mar - 31 Oct daily	10am - 5.30pm
	1 Oct. - Mid Mar. daily	11am - 4pm
Leathad Ard, Isle of Lewis	9 Jun - 23 Aug Tue, Thur, Sat	2 - 6pm
Leckmelm Shrubbery & Arboretum, ...	1 April - 31 October daily	10am - 6pm

Inverewe, Poolewe	Saturday 14 April	9.30am - 5pm
Dundonnell House, Dundonnel, Wester Ross	Thursday 26 Apil	2 - 5pm
Kilcoy Castle, Muir of Ord	Sunday 13 May	2 - 6pm
House of Gruinard, by Laide	Wednesday 30 May	2 - 5pm
Attadale, Strathcarron	Saturday 2 June	2 - 5pm
Dundonnell House, Dundonnel, Wester Ross	Thursday 7 June	2 - 5pm
Brahan, Dingwall	Saturday 9 June	2 - 5.30pm
Novar, Evanton	Sunday 10 June	2.30pm
House of Aigas & Field Centre, By Beauly	Sunday 24 June	2 - 5.30pm
Kilcoy Castle, Muir of Ord	Sunday 1 July	2 - 6pm
House of Aigas & Field Centre, By Beauly	Sunday 22 July	2 - 5.30pm
Dundonnell House, Dundonnel, Wester Ross	Thursday 6 September	2 - 5pm
Inverewe, Poolewe	Sunday 9 September	9.30am - 5pm

1. ABRIACHAN GARDEN NURSERY, Loch Ness Side IV3 6LA
(Mr & Mrs Davidson)
An outstanding garden. Over 4 acres of exciting plantings, with winding paths through native woodlands. Seasonal highlights – hellebores, primulas, meconopsis, hardy geraniums and colour-themed summer beds. Views over Loch Ness. New path to pond through the Bluebell Wood.
Route: on A82 Inverness/Drumnadrochit road, approximately 8 miles south of Inverness.
Admission £2.00.
FEBRUARY to NOVEMBER 9am - dusk
Donation to Scotland's Gardens Scheme

2. AN ACARSAID, Ord, Sleat, Isle of Skye IV44 8QN
(Mrs Eileen MacInnes)
A two acre garden perched on low cliffs above the shore of Loch Eishort with stunning views to the Cuillins. Informal mixed plantings, started in the 1960s, with shrubbery and viewpoint, lawns, borders and scree bed and many cobbled paths.
Route: Take A851 from Broadford or Armadale. Ord is signposted 5 miles from Armadale.
Admission by donation box.
APRIL - OCTOBER 10am - 5.30pm
Donation to Crossroads Care & SGS Charities

3. ATTADALE, Strathcarron IV54 8YX

(Mr & Mrs Ewen Macpherson)

The Gulf Stream and surrounding hills and rocky cliffs create a microclimate for outstanding water gardens, old rhododendrons, unusual trees and fern collection in a geodesic dome. Japanese garden.

Route: on A890 between Strathcarron and South Strome.

Admission £4.50 OAP's £3.00 Children £1.00 &. free

SATURDAY 2 JUNE 2 - 5pm

40% to The Highland Hospice 60% to SGS Charities

1 April - 31 October 10am - 5.30pm Closed Sundays

Donation to Scotland's Gardens Scheme

&. (partial) (in house Saturday 2 June) Tea room

4. BALMEANACH HOUSE, Struan, Isle of Skye IV56 8FH

(Mrs Arlene Macphie)

A formal garden with herbaceous border and bedding: and an azalea/rhododendron walk. To make this garden one third of an acre of croft land was fenced in during the late 1980s and there is now a woodland dell with fairies, three ponds and a shrubbery.

Route: A87 to Sligachan, turn left, Balmeanach is 5 miles north of Struan and 5 miles south of Dunvegan.

Admission By donation box - suggested donation £2.00

END - APRIL - MID OCTOBER WEDNESDAY & SATURDAYS 11am - 4.30pm

40% to SSPCA 60% net to SGS Charities

5. BRAHAN, Dingwall IV7 8EE

(Mr & Mrs A Matheson)

Wild garden, dell with azaleas and rhododendrons. Flower and shrub borders. Arboretum with labelled trees and river walk.

Route: Maryburgh 2 miles. Take A835 west from Maryburgh roundabout.

Admission £3.00 Children free

SATURDAY 9 JUNE 2 - 5.30pm

40% to Highland Hospice 60% net to SGS Charities

 (home made)

6. COILTIE GARDEN, Divach, Drumnadrochit IV3 6XW

(Gillian & David Nelson)

A wooded garden, an amalgamation of a Victorian flower garden abandoned 60 years ago and a walled field with a large moraine. This garden has been made over the past 20 years and development work is still in progress. Many trees, old and new, mixed shrub and herbaceous borders, roses, wall beds, rockery.

Route: off A82 at Drumnadrochit. Take road signposted Divach, uphill 2 miles, past Divach Lodge, 150m.

Admission £2.00 Children free

20 JUNE - 20 JULY DAILY Noon - 7pm

40% to Amnesty International 60% to SGS Charities

&.

7. DUNDONNELL HOUSE, Dundonnell, Wester Ross IV23 2QW

Camelias and magnolias and bulbs in spring, rhodedendrons, and laburnum walk in this ancient walled garden. Delightful new borders for all year colour, centred around one of the oldest yew trees in Scotland. Riverside walk below the peaks of An Teallach in the fine arboretum. Restored Victorian glasshouse compliments the specimen holly and tulip trees.

Route: off A832 between Braemore and Gairloch. Take Badralloch turn for $^1/_2$ mile.

Admission £2.50 Children free

THURSDAY 26 APRIL 2 - 5pm
THURSDAY 7 JUNE 2 - 5pm
THURSDAY 6 SEPTEMBER 2 - 5pm

40% to Breast Cancer Haven 60% net to SGS Charities - April and September openings
40% Fauna & Flora International 60% net to SGS Charities - June opening

♿ (partially) ⛾ (7 June) 26 April and 6 September tea available at Maggie's Tea Room - 4 miles towards Little Loch Broom

---

8. DUNVEGAN CASTLE, Isle of Skye IV55 8WF

Dating from the 13th century and continuously inhabited by the Chiefs of MacLeod, this romantic fortress stronghold occupies a magnificent lochside setting. The gardens, originally laid out in the 18th century, have been extensively replanted and inlcude lochside walks, woodlands and water gardens and a walled garden.

Route: Dunvegan Village 1 mile, 23 miles west of Portree.

Admission: Gardens only: £5.00, OAPs and Students £3.50, Children £3.00
Castle and Gardens: £7.00, OAPs/Students & groups £6.00 Children (5-15) £4.00

MID MARCH - 31 OCT: Daily Castle & Gardens 10am - 5.30pm (last entry 5pm)
1 NOV. - MID MARCH: Daily Castle & Gardens 11am - 4pm (last entry 3.30pm)

Donation to Scotland's Gardens Scheme

⛾ Licensed restaurant, Two craft shops, woollen shop, kilts and country wear shop, clan exhibition, audio-visual theatre, pedigree Highland cattle fold, boat trips to seal colony.

---

9. HOUSE of AIGAS and FIELD CENTRE, by Beauly IV4 7AD

(Sir John and Lady Lister-Kaye)
Aigas has a woodland walk overlooking the Beauly River with a collection of named Victorian specimen trees now being restored and extended with a garden of rockeries, herbaceous borders and shrubberies.

Route: $4^1/_2$ miles from Beauly on A831 Cannich/Glen Affric road.

Admission from £3.00 Children free

SUNDAYS 24 JUNE & 22 JULY 2 - 5.30pm

40% to Highland Hospice 60% net to SGS Charities

⛾ (home made in house) Guided walks on nature trails

10. HOUSE OF GRUINARD, Laide IV22 2NQ
(The Hon Mrs A G Maclay)
Hidden and unexpected garden developed in sympathy with stunning west coast estuary location. Wide variety of herbaceous and shrub borders with water garden and extended wild planting.
Route: on A832 12 miles north of Inverewe and 9 miles south of Dundonnell.
Admission £3.00 Children under 16 free
WEDNESDAY 30 MAY 2 - 5pm
40% to Highland Hospice 60% net to SGS Charities

11. INVEREWE, Poolewe IV22 2LG
(The National Trust for Scotland)
Magnificent 50-acre Highland garden, surrounded by mountains, moorland and sea-loch. Founded from 1862 by Osgood Mackenzie, it now includes a wealth of exotic plants, from Australian tree ferns to Chinese rhododendrons to South African bulbs.
Admission £8.00
(For further price information/concessions please see NTS advert at back of book)
SATURDAY 14 APRIL & SUNDAY 9 SEPTEMBER 9.30am - 5pm
40% to The Gardens Fund of the National Trust for Scotland 60% net to SGS Charities

  (self-service restaurant) Shop

12. KILCOY CASTLE, Muir of Ord IV6 7RX
(Mr & Mrs Nick McAndrew)
16th century castle (not open) surrounded by extensive terraced lawns, walled garden with fine herbaceous and shrub borders, surrounding vegetable garden. Woodland areas with rhododendrons, azaleas and particularly fine mature trees and shrubs. Winner of 'Inverness Courier' 'Large garden of the Year' award 2001, 2002 and 2005.
Route: A9 to Tore roundabout, A832 signed Beauly and Muir of Ord. After one and a half miles, turn right at church signed Kilcoy, entrance is half a mile on left.
Admission £2.50 Children under 12 free
SUNDAYS 13 MAY & 1 JULY 2 - 6pm
40% to Highland Hospice 60% net to SGS Charities

13. LEATHAD ARD, Upper Carloway, Isle of Lewis HS2 9AQ
(Rowena & Stuart Oakley)
A sloping garden view towards East Loch Roag. The garden has evolved as the shelter hedges have grown, dividing the garden into separate areas with bog gardens, herbaceious borders, cutting borders, patio and vegetables.
Route: take A858 from Shawbost to Carloway. First right after entering village (opposite football pitch). First house on right.
Admission Donations welcome
9 JUNE TO 23 AUGUST TUESDAYS, THURSDAYS and SATURDAYS 2 - 6pm
40% to Red Cross 60% net to SGS Charities

14. LECKMELM SHRUBBERY & ARBORETUM, by Ullapool IV23 2RH
(Mr & Mrs Peter Troughton)
The restored 12 acre arboretum, planted in the 1880s, is full of splendid and rare trees, including 2 "Champions", specie rhododendrons, azaleas and shrubs. Warmed by the Gulf Stream, this tranquil woodland garden has alpines, meconopsis, palms, bamboos and winding paths which lead down to the sea.
Route: Situated by the shore of Loch Broom 3 miles south of Ullapool on the A835 Inverness/Ullapool road. Parking in walled garden.
Admission £2.50 Children under 16 free
1 APRIL - 31 OCTOBER 10am - 6pm DAILY
Donation to Scotland's Gardens Scheme and Local Charities

15. NOVAR, Evanton
(Mr & Mrs Ronald Munro Ferguson)
Water gardens with flowering shrubs, trees and plants, especially rhododendrons and azaleas. Large, five acre walled garden with formal 18th century oval pond (restored).
Route: off B817 between Evanton and junction with A836; turn west up Novar Drive.
Admission £3.00 Children free
SUNDAY 10 JUNE 2.30pm
40% to Diabetes Charities   60% net to SGS Charities

 (most areas)

ROXBURGH

District Organiser: **Mrs M D Blacklock,** Stable House, Maxton, St Boswells TD6 0EX

Area Organiser: **Mrs T R Harley**, Estate House, Smailholm TD5 7PH

Treasurer: **Mr Peter Jeary,** Kalemouth, Eckford, Kelso

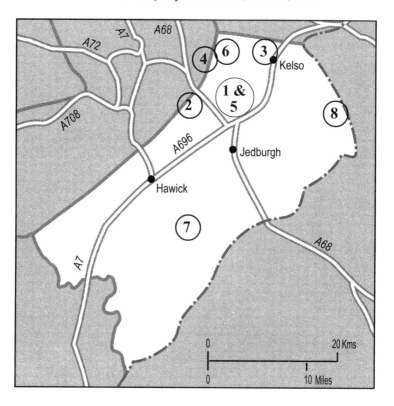

DATES OF OPENING

Floors Castle Walled Garden, Kelso .... All year daily   9.30am - 5pm
Monteviot House, Jedburgh .... 1 April - 31 October daily   12 - 5pm

Mertoun, St Boswells .... Sat & Sun 10 & 11 February 11am - 4pm
Floors Castle, Kelso - Journey of the Snowdrop
                    Workshop .... Thur. 15 Feb.   Pre-book 01573 223333
Smailholm Village Gardens, ... Sunday 17 June   2 - 6pm
Floors Castle, Kelso - Gardeners' Festival .... Sat & Sun 7 & 8 July   11am - 5pm
Gardens in Buccleuch Chase, St Boswells .... Sunday 8 July   2 - 5.30pm
The Ask Organic Garden, Jedburgh .... Wednesday 11 July   6 - 9pm
West Leas, Bonchester Bridge .... Sunday 15 July   2 - 6pm
Yetholm Village .... Sunday 22 July   2 - 6pm

1. THE ASK ORGANIC GARDEN, Jedburgh TD9 9TP
Within Woodside Walled Garden

(The ASK Organic Garden Club)

Stroll through this ¹/₂ acre organic garden set in a tranquil Victorian walled garden and enjoy all its delicate evening fragrances. Sip a glass of organic wine and enjoy interesting nibbles prepared with fresh ingredients from the garden. Scotland's first organic demonstration garden contains planting ideas to attract birds and beneficial insects, potagers showing vegetables and herbs to please both eye and palate. Slug barrier and weed eradication trials, a trained mixed fruit hedge, wild flower herbaceous border, composting demonstrations and much more.

Route: 3 miles north of Jedburgh, east off A68 on to B6400. Woodside Walled Garden is ¹/₂ mile on left.

Admission £5.00 (including glass of wine and nibbles) Children free

WEDNESDAY 11 JULY 6 - 9pm

40% to ASK Organic Garden Club   60% net to SGS Charities

♿ ✿ (in Woodside Walled Garden)   Wine and nibbles

---

2. GARDENS IN BUCCLEUCH CHASE, St Boswells TD6 0HB

(Mr & Mrs Kennedy, Mr & Mrs Dawson, Mrs Watson, Mr & Mrs Sealy, Mr & Mrs Highley, Mr & Mrs Wilson, Mr & Mrs Bertram, Mr & Mrs Warner)

This is an interesting range of gardens showing what can be achieved in a new attractive housing development within 4 years. Each garden reflects its owners' enthusiasm, whether it be love of individual plants or overall visual effect.

Route: A68 to St Boswells. Turn onto A699 to Selkirk Gardens 200 yards on right.

Admission £3.00

SUNDAY 8 JULY 2 - 5.30pm

40% between Samaritans and Marie Curie Cancer Care   60% net to SGS Charities

♿ (partly) ✿

---

3. FLOORS CASTLE, Kelso

(The Duke of Roxburghe)

The largest inhabited house in Scotland enjoys glorious views across parkland, the River Tweed & the Cheviot Hills. Woodland garden, riverside and woodland walks, formal French style Millennium Parterre and the traditional walled garden. The walled garden contains colourful herbaceous borders, vinery & peach house, and in keeping with the tradition, the kitchen garden still supplies vegetables and soft fruit for the castle.

Admission Walled Garden (honesty box)

Castle & Grounds: Adults £6.50 Seniors/Students £5.50 Children (5 - 16) £3.50 Under 5's free
Grounds: Adults £3.00 Seniors/Students £1.50 Children (under 16) free

THURSDAY 15 FEB. - Journey of the Snowdrop (Pre-booked workshop Tel. 01573 223333)

SATURDAY & SUNDAY 7 & 8 JULY 11am - 5pm - Gardeners' Festival.

All year daily Walled Garden, Garden Centre and Terrace cafe 9.30am - 5pm

Easter then daily 1 May - 28 October Castle 11am - 5pm (last admission to castle 4.30pm.)
Enquiries 01573 223333 *www.floorscastle.com*
Donation to Scotland's Gardens Scheme

☕ (with coffee shop specialising in homemade dishes prepared by the Duke's chef)
Garden Centre, Children's Adventure Playground

---

4. MERTOUN GARDENS, St Boswells
(The Duke of Sutherland)
Snowdrop day. Circular walks lead over drifts of SNOWDROPS and takes you on through the garden and arboretum, past the 16ᵗʰ century dovecote and into the extensive walled garden.
Route: 1¹/₂ miles from St Boswells on the B6404 to Kelso
Admission £3.00 Children free
SATURDAY & SUNDAY 10 & 11 FEBRUARY 11am - 4pm
40% to Mertoun Kirk   60% net to SGS Charities

5. MONTEVIOT, Jedburgh
Monteviot garden lies along a steep rise above the Teviot valley, a setting which adds a sense of drama to its many outstanding features. From the box-hedged herb garden in front of the House with its unique and breathtaking view of the river below, down through the sheltered terraced rose-garden, which slopes down between curved borders of herbaceous plants and shrubs to a broad stone landing stage. In the Water Garden, three islands are linked by elegant wooden bridges and planted with a variety of bog and damp-loving plants. New for 2007 is the cascading water feature through the arboretum.
Route: turn off A68, 3 miles north of Jedburgh B6400.
Admission £3.50 Children under 16 free
1 APRIL – 31 OCTOBER DAILY 12 noon – 5pm (last entry 4pm)
Donation to Scotland's Gardens Scheme

♿ (partially)

6. SMAILHOLM VILLAGE GARDENS
This attractive village provides a wealth of interest in several delightful gardens ranging in style and size from historic houses to traditional cottages. They include the plantsman's garden, woodland areas, herbaceous borders, alpine troughs and organic vegetables - something for everyone.
Route: B6397 between Kelso and Earlston.
Admission £3.00 Children free Ticket and maps from Village Hall.
SUNDAY 17 JUNE 2 - 6pm
40% to Smailholm Village Hall 60% net to SGS Charities

♿ (some) 🌼 (wide range of home grown plants) ☕ (delicious home made)
Children's woodland play area

Our website, www.gardensofscotland.org, provides information on Scotland's Gardens Scheme and the gardens that open for us.

The site will be re-designed in the course of 2007

---

7. WEST LEAS, Bonchester Bridge
(Mr and Mrs Robert Laidlaw)
The visitor to West Leas can share in the exciting and dramatic project on a grand scale still in the making. At its core is a passion for plants allied to a love and understanding of the land in which they are set. Collections of perennials and shrubs, many in temporary holding quarters, lighten up the landscape to magical effect. New landscaped water features, bog garden and extensive new shrub planting. A recently planted orchard, with underplantings of spring bulbs, demonstrates that the productive garden can be highly ornamental.
Route: Signed off the Jedburgh/Bonchester Bridge Road.
Admission £3.00 Children free
SUNDAY 15 JULY 2 - 6pm
40% to MacMillan Cancer Relief, Border Appeal 60% net to SGS Charities

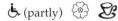 (partly)

8. YETHOLM VILLAGE GARDENS
Copsewood, Morebattle Road (Fraser & Alison Nimmo)
Almond Cottage, 2 Yew Tree Lane (Jim & Isabel Cockburn
5 Yew Tree Lane (Peter & Margaret Boyd)
Hazeldean, Yew Tree Road (Stan & Liz Brown)
Brackenrigg, Yew Tree Road (John & Wilma Thomson)
Rosebank, Venchen Road (Gavin & Barbara Harding)
The Old Manse, Venchen Road (Alistair Turnbull)
The Hall House, High Street (Mike & Anne Marsh)
Amat, High Street (Margaret & Dennis Harding)
Cheviot View, High Street (Susan & John White)
Staerough View (Peter & Tricia Duncan)
Situated at the north end of the Pennine Way in the dramatic setting of the foothills of the Cheviots, Town Yetholm offers visitors the chance to walk through several delightful gardens planted in a variety of styles and reflecting many distinctive horticultural interests. The short walking distance between the gardens provides the added advantage of being able to enjoy the magnificence of the surrounding landscape to include 'Staerough' and 'The Curr' which straddle both the Bowmont and Halterburn Valleys where evidence of ancient settlements remain.
Route: South of Kelso take the B6352 to Town Yetholm.
Admission £3.00 includes all gardens Children under 10 Free
Tickets sold on the Village Green
SUNDAY 22 JULY 2 - 6pm
30% to Yetholm Primary School 10% to Yetholm Floral Gateway 60% net to SGS Charities

(and home baking, garden produce on Village Green) (home baked - served in the Youth Hall) Local Artists - wood turned products, sketches and cards Brick-a-brack Book stall

STEWARTRY OF KIRKCUDBRIGHT

District Organiser: **Mrs C Cathcart,** Culraven, Borgue, Kirkcudbright DG6 4SG

Area Organisers: **Mrs P Addison,** Killeron Farm, Gatehouse of Fleet,
Castle Douglas DG7 2BS

Mrs W N Dickson, Chipperkyle, Kirkpatrick Durham, Castle Douglas
DG7 3EY

Mrs M R C Gillespie, Danevale Park, Crossmichael, Castle Douglas
DG7 2LP

Mrs W B Kirkpatrick, Rough Hills, Sandyhills, Dumfries DG5 4NZ

Mrs B Marshall, Cairnview, Carsphairn DG7 3TQ

Mrs J F Mayne, Hazelfield House, Auchencairn, Castle Douglas
DG7 1RF

Mrs M McIlvenna, Brae Neuk, Balmaclellan, Castle Douglas DG7 3QS

Mrs S Purdie, The Old Kirk, Hardgate, Castle Douglas DG7 3LD

Mrs C V Scott, 14 Castle Street, Kircudbright DG6 4JA

Treasurer: **Mr P Phillips,** The Old Manse, Old Ferry Road, Crossmichael
Castle Douglas DG7 3AT

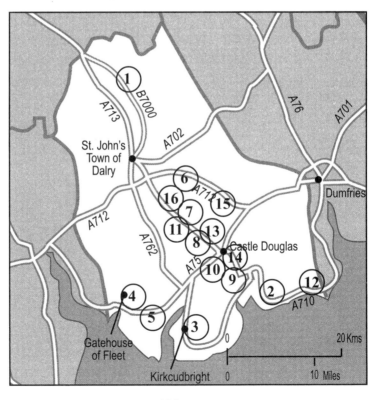

DATES OF OPENING

Arndarroch, St John's Town of Dalry	July - September by appt.	
Barnhourie Mill, Colvend	May - Oct by appt.	
Cally Gardens, Gatehouse of Fleet	Easter Sat - last Sun Sept	
	Tues - Fri	2.30 - 5.30pm
	Sat & Sun	10am -5.30pm
Carleton Croft, Borgue	July to August by appt.	
Corsock House, Castle Douglas	Apr - June by appt.	
	(and for Autumn Colours)	
Danevale Park, Crossmichael	To 1 June by appt.	
Southwick House, Dumfries	Monday 25 - Friday 29 June	

Danevale Park, Crossmichael (Snowdrops)	To be announced	
Walton Park, Castle Douglas	Sunday 6 May	2 - 5pm
Danevale Park, Crossmichael (Bluebells)	Sunday 20 May	2 - 5pm
Corsock House, Castle Douglas	Sunday 27 May	2 - 5pm
Cally Gardens, Gatehouse of Fleet	Sunday 10 June	10am - 5.30pm
The Old Manse, Crossmichael	Sunday 17 June	2 - 5pm
Southwick House, Dumfries	Sunday 24 June	2 - 5pm
Broughton House Garden, Kirkcudbright	Sunday 1 July	12 - 5pm
Threave Garden, Castle Douglas	Sunday 8 July	9.30am - 5.30pm
Crossmichael Gardens, Crossmichael	Sunday 15 July	2 - 5pm
Millhouse, Rhonehouse	Sunday 22 July	2 - 5pm
The Mill House, Gelston	Sunday 22 July	2 - 5pm
Arndarroch, St John's Town of Dalry	Sunday 29 July	2 - 5pm
Square Point, Crossmichael	Sunday 5 August	2 - 5pm
Waterside , Crossmichael	Sunday 5 August	2 - 5pm
Cally Gardens, Gatehouse of Fleet	Sunday 12 August	10am - 5.30pm
Arndarroch, St John's Town of Dalry	Sat & Sun 8 & 9 September	2 - 5pm

1. ARNDARROCH , St John's Town of Dalry DG7 3UD
(Annikki and Matt Lindsay)

A young $2^{1}/_{4}$ acre garden created since 1991 on a windswept hillside overlooking Kendoon Loch. A great variety of trees, some species roses and shrubs have been underplanted with herbaceous plants. Small kitchen garden. Collections of oriental and medicinal plants. Also a collection of over 20 different bamboos. A small woodland was planted in 2000. The aim has been to create a semi-natural, wildlife friendly environment.

Route: about 5 miles from St John's Town of Dalry or Carsphairn on the B7000. Follow signs to the Youth Hostel.

Admission £3.00 Children free

SUNDAY 29 JULY 2 - 5pm

SATURDAY 8 & SUNDAY 9 SEPTEMBER 2 - 5pm

Also open by appointment July to September Tel. 01644 460640

40% to Dumfries & Galloway Canine Rescue Centre 60% net to SGS Charities

 (partly) ♦ ✿ ☕ (In July only - £2.00)

2. BARNHOURIE MILL, Colvend DG5 4PU
(Dr M R Paton)
Flowering shrubs and trees, dwarf conifers and an especially fine collection of rhododendron species.
Route: A710 from Dumfries. Dalbeattie 5 miles.
Admission £3.00 Children free
MAY - OCTOBER BY APPOINTMENT for groups and individuals Tel. 01387 780269
40% to Scottish Wildlife Trust 60% net to SGS Charities

 (partly)

---

3. BROUGHTON HOUSE GARDEN, Kirkcudbright DG6 4JX
(National Trust for Scotland)
Small fascinating garden that belonged to E A Hornel - artist, collector and Glasgow boy. Full of Colour, mostly herbaceous, old apple trees, greenhouse with old pelargonium varieties, fruit and vegetable garden.
Route: on High Street, Kirkcudbright
Admission £3.00 Children free
SUNDAY 1 JULY 12 - 5pm
40% to NTS Gardens 60% net to SGS Charities

   House open

---

4. CALLY GARDENS, Gatehouse of Fleet DG7 2DJ
(Mr Michael Wickenden)
A specialist nursery in a fine 2.7 acre, 18th century walled garden with old vinery and bothy, all surrounded by the Cally Oak woods. Our collection of 3,500 varieties can be seen and a selection will be available pot-grown, especially rare herbaceous perennials. Forestry nature trails nearby.
Route: from Dumfries take the Gatehouse turning off A75 and turn left, through the Cally Palace Hotel Gateway from where the gardens are well signposted.
Admission £2.50.
10 JUNE & 12 AUGUST SUNDAY 10am - 5.30pm
Also 7 April - 30 September Tuesday – Friday 2–5.30pm,
Saturday & Sunday 10am–5.30pm. Closed Mondays.
40% to Save the Children Fund 60% net to SGS Charities

---

5. CARLETON CROFT, Borgue DG6 4ST
(Mr and Mrs D J Hartley)
Cottage garden with well stocked and interesting herbaceous beds, shrubs, trees, tubs and baskets. Created for wildlife and the pleasure of gardening.
Route: on the B272 between Borgue and Gatehouse of Fleet.
Admission By Donation.
JULY AND AUGUST BY APPOINTMENT Tel. 01557 870447
40% to Wigtownshire Animal Welfare Association 60% net to SGS Charities

---

6. CORSOCK HOUSE, Castle Douglas DG7 3DJ

(Mr & Mrs M L Ingall)

Rhododendrons, woodland walks with temples, water gardens and loch. David Bryce turretted "Scottish Baronial" house in background.

<u>Route:</u> Dumfries 14 miles, Castle Douglas 10 miles, Corsock half mile on A712.

<u>Admission</u> £3.00 Children Free

SUNDAY 27 MAY 2 - 5pm

Also April to June and for autumn colours by appointment. Tel. 01644 440250

40% to Corsock & Kirkpatrick Durham Kirk 60% net to SGS Charities

7. CROSSMICHAEL GARDENS

19 Rhonepark Crescent DG7 3BN (Geoff Packard)

Quarter acre garden on a south west facing slope. Extensive rockery, herbaceous border, ornamental grasses and mature conifers on three levels.

3 Main Street DG7 3AU (K Hutchison)

Well established flower arranger's garden.

5 Main Street DG7 3AU (Mrs Jeanie Galloway)

Small village garden with a mixture of perennials and annuals

<u>Route:</u> village 3 miles north of Castle Douglas on the A713. Follow signs in village.

<u>Admission</u> £3.00 Children Free.

SUNDAY 15 JULY 2 - 5pm

40% to Galloway Mountain Rescue 60% net to SGS Charities

 (at 3 Main Street and 4 Main Street) (in village hall)

8. DANEVALE PARK, Crossmichael DG7 2LP

(Mrs M R C Gillespie)

Open for snowdrops. Mature garden with woodland walks alongside the River Dee. Walled garden.

<u>Route:</u> A713. Crossmichael 1 mile, Castle Douglas 2 miles.

<u>Admission</u> £2.50 Children free

SUNDAY 18 FEB for Snowdrops 2 - 5pm

40% to Crossmichael Village Hall 60% net to SGS Charities (Snowdrop Opening)

SUNDAY 20 MAY for Bluebells 2 - 5pm

40% to Edinburgh Erskine Home 60% net to SGS Charities (Bluebells Opening)

Also until 1 June by appointment Tel. 01556 670223

 (in house £2.00)

9. THE MILL HOUSE, Gelston DG7 1SH

(Magnus Ramsay)

A collection of plants for small gardens.

<u>Route:</u> entrance to village of Gelston from Castle Douglas at the 30 mile speed limit sign on B727.

<u>Admission</u> £3.00 Children free

JOINT OPENING WITH MILLHOUSE, RHONEHOUSE

SUNDAY 22 JULY 2 - 5pm

40% to Afghan Schools Trust 60% net to SGS Charities

 (at Gelston Village Hall)

10. MILLHOUSE, Rhonehouse DG7 1RZ
(Bill Hean)
Small garden, mainly herbaceous and alpines. Vegetable garden.
Route: signs in village of Rhonehouse, just off A75 west of Castle Douglas.
Admission £3.00 Children free
JOINT OPENING WITH THE MILL HOUSE, GELSTON
SUNDAY 22 JULY 2 - 5pm
40% to Buittle & Kelton Church 60% net to SGS Charities

 (at Gelston Village Hall)

---

11. THE OLD MANSE, Crossmichael DG7 3AT
(Mr and Mrs Peter Phillips)
Roses, shrubs, azaleas, herbaceous, rock garden in a constantly developing working
garden created over the past decade. Splendid view to River Dee.
Route: on A713 Castle Douglas/Ayr on edge of Crossmichael Village.
Admission £3.00 Children free
SUNDAY 17 JUNE 2 - 5pm
40% to Abbeyfield Stewartry Society Ltd. 60% net to SGS Charities

 (from our own stock) (in Crossmichael Village Hall)

---

12. SOUTHWICK HOUSE, Southwick DG2 8AH
(Mr & Mrs R H L Thomas)
Traditional formal walled garden with lily ponds, herbaceous borders, shrubs,
vegetables, fruit and greenhouses. Fine trees and lawns through which flows the
Southwick burn. New developments in water garden.
Route: on A710 near Caulkerbush. Dalbeattie 7 miles, Dumfries 17 miles.
Admission £3.00 Children free
SUNDAY 24 JUNE 2 - 5pm
ALSO MONDAY 25 JUNE - FRIDAY 29 JUNE - Honesty Box
20% to Perennial (GRBS) 20% to Loch Arthur 60% net to SGS Charities

---

13. SQUARE POINT, Crossmichael DG7 2LL
(Lt Col E W Jenno)
Garden of roughly two thirds of an acre, put down entirely to beds and borders.
Contains hundreds of different shrubs and hardy perennial plants.
Route: 1$^{1}/_{2}$ miles south of Crossmichael on A713.
Admission £3.00 Children free
JOINT OPENING WITH WATERSIDE, CROSSMICHAEL
SUNDAY 5 AUGUST 2 - 5pm
40% to Crossmichael & Parton Church 60% net to SGS Charities

(in Crossmichael Church Hall)

---

14. THREAVE GARDEN, Castle Douglas DG7 1RX
(The National Trust for Scotland)
Home of the Trust's School of Practical Gardening. Spectacular daffodils in spring, colourful herbaceous borders in summer, striking autumn trees and heather garden.
Route: A75, one mile west of Castle Douglas.
Admission £6.00 Children & OAPs £4.75 Family £14.50
SUNDAY 8 JULY 9.30am - 5.30pm
40% to The Gardens Fund of The National Trust for Scotland 60% net to SGS Charities

 Plant centre

---

15. WALTON PARK, Castle Douglas DG7 3DD
(Mr Jeremy Brown)
Walled garden, gentian borders. Flowering shrubs, rhododendrons and azaleas.
Route: B794 to Corsock, three and a half miles from A75.
Admission £3.00 Children free
SUNDAY 6 MAY 2 - 5pm
40% to Corsock & Kirkpatrick Durham Church 60% net to SGS Charities

---

16. WATERSIDE, Crossmichael DG7 3BG
(Mrs K Anderson)
A garden created since 1988 to give year round variety and colour.
Route: $^1/_2$ a mile north of Crossmichael on A713.
Admission £3.00 Children free
JOINT OPENING WITH SQARE POINT, CROSSMICHAEL DG7 2LL
SUNDAY 5 AUGUST 2 - 5pm
40% to Crossmichael & Parton Church 60% net to SGS Charities

  (in Crossmichael Church Hall)

STIRLING

Joint District Organisers: **Maud Crawford**, St Blane's House, Dunblane FK15 OER
     Lesley Stein, Southwood, Southfield Crescent, Stirling
     FK8 2JQ

Area Organisers: **Carola Campbell**, Kilbryde Castle, Doune FK15 3HN
     Jean Gore, Braehead, 69 Main Street, Doune FK16 8BW
     Fleur McIntosh, 8 Albert Place, Stirling FK8 2QL
     Sue Stirling-Aird, Old Kippenross, Dunblane FK15 OLQ
     Helen Younger, Old Leckie, Gargunnock FK8 3BN

Treasurer   **John McIntyre**, 18 Scott Brae, Kippen FK8 3DL

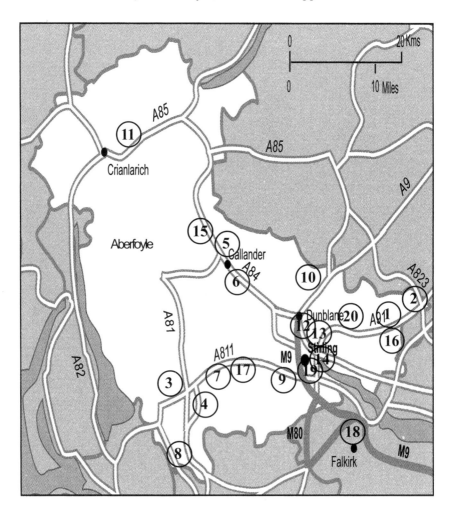

DATES OF OPENING

14 Glebe Crescent, Tillicoultry	By appointment	Tel. 01259 750484
Arndean, By Dollar	Mid May - end June by appointment	
	Tel. 01259 742527	
Callander Lodge, Callander	April - end August by appointment	
	Tel. 01877 330136	
Culbuie, Buchlyvie	May - Oct. Tuesdays 1 - 5pm	
	Groups by appt.	Tel. 01360 850232
Gargunnock House, Gargunnock	Feb - 11 Mar Suns/Weds 10.30am - 3.30pm	
	Apr - mid Jun, Sept./Oct. Weds. 2 - 5pm	
	and by appointment	Tel. 01786 860392
Kilbryde Castle, Dunblane	By appointment	Tel. 01786 824897
Milseybank, Bridge of Allan	By appointment	Tel. 01786 833866
The Steading, Hillhead	Groups by appt.	Tel. 01786 870710
Thorntree, Arnprior	By appointment	Tel.01786 870710

Milseybank, Bridge of Allan	Sunday 15 April	1 - 5pm
Auchmar, Drymen	Sunday 22 April	2 - 5pm
The Pass House, Kilmahog	Sunday 29 April	2 - 5pm
Kilbryde Castle, Dunblane	Sunday 13 May	2 - 5pm
Gargunnock House, Gargunnock	Sunday 20 May	2 - 5pm
Yellowcraig Wood, Stirling District	Sunday 20 May	11am - 4pm
Lochdochart, Crianlarich	Sunday 27 May	12 - 4pm
Touch, Stirling	Sunday 27 May	2 - 5pm
Duntreath Castle, Blanefield	Sunday 3 June	2 - 5pm
Kilbryde Castle, Dunblane	Sunday 10 June	2 - 5pm
The Steading, Hillhead	Sunday 10 June	1 - 5pm
Plaka and other Bridge of Allan Gardens	Sunday 17 June	2 - 5pm
Cambusmore & other gardens, Callander	Sunday 24 June	1 - 5pm
Southwood, Stirling	Sunday 8 July	2 - 5pm
14 Glebe Crescent, Tillicoultry	Sunday 22 July	1 - 5pm
The Tors, Falkirk	Sunday 29 July	2 - 6pm
Burnbrae, Killearn	Sunday 5 August	2 - 5pm
Thorntree, Arnprior	Sunday 19 August	2 - 5pm

1. 14 GLEBE CRESCENT, Tillicoultry FK13 5PB

(Jim & Joy McCorgray)

Half acre beautifully designed plantsman's garden with specialist areas. Japanese, ornamental grasses, bonsai, conifer and perfumed gardens. Koi carp pool. Woodland area in spring offers paticular interest. As featured on 'The Beechgrove Garden' and in 'Gorgeous Gardens' and 'Garden Answers' magazines.

<u>Route:</u> A91 St Andrews/Stirling road; east end of Tillicoultry; yellow arrow at Glebe Crescent.

<u>Admission</u> £3.00 Senior Citizens £2.50 Children free

SUNDAY 22 JULY 1 - 5pm

Also by appointment Tel. 01259 750484

40% to The New Struan School for Autism Appeal 60% net to SGS Charities

♿ ✿ (home grown) ☕ (home made)

2. ARNDEAN, by Dollar FK14 7NH
(Sir Robert & Lady Stewart)
Flowering shrubs, rhododendrons, azaleas, woodland walk.
Route: off A977 and A91
Admission Adults £3.50
MID MAY - END JUNE by appointment Tel: 01259 742527
40% to Strathcarron Hospice 60% net to SGS Charities

3. AUCHMAR, Drymen G63 0AG NEW
(Duke & Duchess of Montrose)
Designed by the late Mary Duchess of Montrose in 1935. 5$^1/_2$ acres of daffodils and
rhododendrons of different varieties. Deep glen and waterfall with woodland walks.
Recently renovated walled garden with shrubs and herbaceous borders. Spectacular view
of Loch Lomond.
Route: from Erskine Bridge - A811 to Drymen, from Stirling - A811 to Drymen, from
Glasgow - A809 to Drymen, from Drymen - B837 2$^1/_2$ miles.
Admission £4.00 Senior Citizens £2.00 Children free
SUNDAY 22 APRIL 2 - 5pm
40% to The Preshal Trust 60% net to SGS Charities

 (partly)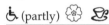

4. BURNBRAE, Killearn G63 9NB
(Mrs Russell Bruce)
Herbaceous, excellent lawn, interesting layout, varied shrubs, mature trees, glen with
burn.
Route: A875 goes through Killearn, Kirkhouse Road sign.
Admission £3.00 Children free
SUNDAY 5 AUGUST 2 - 5pm
40% toCrossroads 60% net to SGS Charities

  SNYO will play on terrace

5. CALLANDER LODGE, Leny Feus, Callander FK17 8AS
(Miss Caroline Penney)
Victorian garden laid out in 1863. Four acres of mature trees, shrubs, herbaceous and
rose borders. Waterfall pool. Fern grotto. Bog garden and water garden. Woodland
walk. Vegetable garden.
Route: A84 west through Callander, turn right at sign for Leny Feus. Garden is at end on
left.
Admission £3.00
APRIL - END AUGUST by appointment Tel. 01877 330136
40% to Camphill Blair Drummond Trust   60% net to SGS Charities

6. CAMBUSMORE FK17 8DF (and other Callander Gardens)
(Captain & Mrs Neil Baillie Hamilton & others)
A diverse and interesting selection of gardens including small cottage gardens and the larger garden at Cambusmore which is set in 3 acres and includes a large formal walled garden, shrub border and woodland walk.
Route: prominent entrance gates 1 mile east of Callander on A84. Map/entry ticket to all gardens can be purchased at any of the open gardens.
Admission £3.50 OAP's £3.00 Children free
SUNDAY 24 JUNE 1 - 5pm
40% to Callander Youth Project   60% net to SGS Charities

7. CULBUIE, Buchlyvie FK8 3NY
(Ian & Avril Galloway)
Spring collection of rhododendrons, azaleas, narcissi, bluebells, primulas and meconopsis. Woodland walk with new planting. Early summer magnolias, cornus and viburnums. Colourful perennial borders. Wild flower meadow. Good autumn colour. Lots of interest throughout this 5 acre garden with splendid views to Ben Lomond and the surrounding hills.
Route: take the A811 to Buchlyvie, turn up Culbowie Road and 'Culbuie' is almost at the top of the hill on the right.
Admission £3.00
MAY to OCTOBER TUESDAYS 1 - 5pm
Groups by appointment Tel. 01360 850232
20% to Macmillan Cancer Relief Fund 20% to Preshal Trust 60% net to SGS Charities

8. DUNTREATH CASTLE, Blanefield G63 9AJ
(Sir Archibald & Lady Edmonstone)
Extensive gardens with mature and new plantings. Landscaped lake, water and bog gardens. Formal garden, rhododendrons and woodland walk. 15th century keep and chapel.
Route: A81 north of Glasgow between Blanefield and Killearn.
Admission £3.00 Children free
SUNDAY 3 JUNE 2 - 5pm
40% to Riding for the Disabled 60% net to SGS Charities

  (home made) 'As new' stall Pipe band Falconry display

Our website, www.gardensofscotland.org, provides information on Scotland's Gardens Scheme and the gardens that open for us.

The site will be re-designed in the course of 2007

141

9. GARGUNNOCK HOUSE, Gargunnock FK8 3AZ
(by kind permission of Gargunnock Trustees)
Five acres of mature rhododendrons, azaleas, unusual flowering shrubs and
wonderful trees with glorious autumn colour.
Route: 5 miles west of Stirling on A811.
1 FEB. - 11 MAR. SUNS &WEDS 10.30am - 3.30pm SNOWDROP FESTIVAL
Tour to house, walled garden area, doocot and main garden
Admission Adults £2.00 Children free
SUNDAY 20 MAY 2 - 5pm SPRING OPENING
April - Mid June and in Sept. & Oct. Wednesdays 2 - 5pm
Also by appointment Tel. 01786 860392
Admission Adults £3.00 Children free
40% to Childrens Hospice Association (Scotland)   60% net to SGS Charities

  (on 20 May)

---

10. KILBRYDE CASTLE, Dunblane, Perthshire FK15 3HN
(Sir James & Lady Campbell & Jack Fletcher)
Traditional Scottish baronial house rebuilt 1877 to replace building dating from 1461.
Partly mature gardens with additions and renovations since 1970. Lawns overlooking
Ardoch Burn with wood and water garden.
Route: three miles from Dunblane and Doune, off the A820 between Dunblane and
Doune. On Garden Scheme days, signposted from A820.
Admission £3.00 Young children free
SUNDAY 13 MAY 2 - 5pm
SUNDAY 10 JUNE 2 - 5pm
Also by appointment Tel. 01786 824897
20% to Leighton Library 20% to Strathcarron Hospice 60% net to SGS Charities

 (partly)   (refreshments, stalls and toilets on Sunday 13 May only)

---

11. LOCHDOCHART, Crianlarich FK20 8Q
(John & Seona Christie of Lochdochart)
Walled garden - fruit, flowers and vegetables. Mature policy woods - rhododendrons
and azaleas. Picnic beach by Loch Iubhair, bring your picnic lunch.
Route: A85, 4 miles east of Crianlarich. Take Oban Road, over hill Lixtill garage - 7
miles from garage Lochdochart 2 Stone pillars on north side of road.
Admission £4.00 Children free
SUNDAY 27 MAY 12 - 4pm
40% to Crianlarich Village Hall 60% net to SGS Charities

  (and produce stall)

12. MILSEYBANK, Bridge of Allan FK9 4NB
(Murray & Sheila Airth)
Steeply sloping garden with outstanding views, terraced for ease of access. Woodland with bluebells, rhododendrons, magnolias and camellias.
Route: Situated on the A9, 1 mile from junction 11, M9 and $^1/_4$ mile from Bridge of Allan. Milseybank is at the top of the lane at Lecropt Nursery and 250 yards from Bridge of Allan train station. Lecropt Kirk is $^3/_4$ mile from M9 and $^1/_2$ mile from Bridge of Allan. Parking at Lecropt Kirk, disabled parking only at house.
Admission £3.00 Children free
SUNDAY 15 APRIL 1 - 5pm
Also by appointment Tel. 01786 833866 (manned answerphone)
40% to Strathcarron Hospice 60% net to SGS Charities

 (at Lecropt Kirk)

13. PLAKA, Pendreich Rd, Bridge of Allan FK9 4LY (and other Bridge of Allan gardens)
(Malcolm & Ann Shaw)
$^1/_2$ acre of semi-terraced gardens divided into outdoor rooms with wild spaces. In addition, there are rhododendrons, perennials and interesting stone features.
Route: follow signs for Bridge of Allan golf club.
Admission Adults £3.00 Children free
SUNDAY 17 JUNE 2 - 5pm
40% to Strathcarron Hospice, 60% net to SGS Charities

14. SOUTHWOOD, Southfield Crescent, Stirling FK8 2JQ
(John & Lesley Stein)
New town garden redesigned in 1987. $^3/_4$ acre of mixed planting including herbacous borders and lavender bed. Interesting specimen trees.
Route: from city centre signed from Carlton Cinema. From south, signed from St Ninian's Road. From west & north, signed from Drummond Place.
Admission £3.50 Children free
SUNDAY 8 JULY 2 - 5pm
40% to Strathcarron Hospice 60% net to SGS Charities

  (s) (cream) Home baking stall

15. THE PASS HOUSE, Kilmahog, Callander FK17 8HD
(Dr & Mrs D Carfrae)
Well planted medium sized garden with steep banks down to swift river. Garden paths not steep. Camellias, rhododendrons, azaleas, alpines and shrubs.
Route: 2 miles from Callander on A84 to Lochearnhead.
Admission £3.00 Children free
SUNDAY 29 APRIL 2 - 5pm
40% to Crossroads Care Attendant Scheme 60% net to SGS Charities

(partly)

16. THE STEADING, Hillhead FK14 7JT

(Fiona and David Chapman)

Situated in rural countryside at the foot of the Ochil Hills, this beautiful $2^1/_2$ acre south facing garden was started 14 years ago and is continually developing. Curvaceous paths meander through a variety of terraced beds, laburnum arch, rockeries and ponds planted with a wide range of seasonal plants and species trees to give all year colour and interest.

Route: take the A823 (towards Dunfermline) at the Yetts o'Muckhart junction A91/A823 on left at 40mph sign

Admission £3.00 OAP's £2.00 Children free

SUNDAY 10 JUNE 1 - 5pm

Also groups welcomed by appointment Tel. 01259 781559

20% to Muckhart Parish Church 20% Muckhart Parish Amenity Soc. 60% net to SGS Charities

---

17. THORNTREE, Arnprior FK8 3EY

(Mark & Carol Seymour)

Charming cottage garden with flower beds around courtyard. Apple walk, fern garden and Saltire garden. Lovely views from Ben Lomond to Ben Ledi. Pretty Primrose bank on drive in April.

Route: A811. In Arnprior take Fintry Road, Thorntree is second on right.

Admission £3.00 Children free

SUNDAY 19 AUGUST 2 - 5pm

Also by appointment Tel. 01786 870710

40% to Bannockburn Group RDA 60% net to SGS Charities

 (permanent)   (cream) Cake stall

---

18. THE TORS, Falkirk FK1 5LG

(Dr & Mrs D M Ramsay)

A town garden of 1 acre, the Tors has a formal area to the front of the Victorian House and a larger sloped garden to the rear with borders, a small orchard and a wild area at the top. At the side of the house lies a secret woodland garden with hostas and ferns. Species rhododendrons and unusual trees, including 7 Chinese paperbark maples which are the main attraction of this property.

Route: from west end take B803 via Cockburn Street, Hodge Street, High Station Road and Glen Brae. The garden is 100 yards from Falkirk High Station via steps to Slamannan Road.

Admission £3.00 OAP's £2.00 Children free

SUNDAY 29 JULY 2 - 5pm

40% to Strathcaron Hospice 60% net to SGS Charities

  Log sculptures and stone ornaments

19. TOUCH, Stirling FK8 3AP

(Angus Watson)

Exceptionally fine Georgian House. Walled garden with herbaceous and shrub borders, specie and dwarf rhododendrons, magnolias and interesting shrubs. Woodland walk.

Route: west from Stirling on A811 then take Cambusbarron Road.

Admission £3.00 Children free House £2.00

SUNDAY 27 MAY 2 - 5pm

40% to Strathcarron Hospice 60% net to SGS Charities

 (small)

---

20. YELLOWCRAIG WOOD, BLUEBELL WALK, Stirling District NEW

(Mrs Rosemary Leckie)

70 acres of ancient woodland with a mixture of trees including oak, ash, birch, beech, gean, rowan, Scots pines and larches. Carpets of bluebells. Beautiful views from 2 Crags, Witches Crag and Yellow Crag (bring binoculars). Lower part of wood on very sleep hill.

Route: From the Causewayhead roundabout, take the B998 passing the Wallace Monument on your right. Turn left just before the next roundabout and go straight along this road, passing Logie Kirk on your right. Further on there is parking on the left side of this road opposite the ruins of the Old Logie Kirk. The entrance to Yellowcraig Wood will be signposted. You can also park after 12.15pm at the Logie Kirk car park and continue walking up the road to the Wood.

Admission £3.00 Young children free

SUNDAY 20 MAY 11am - 4pm

40% to CHAS 60% net to SGS Charities

Our website, www.gardensofscotland.org, provides information on Scotland's Gardens Scheme and the gardens that open for us.

The site will be re-designed in the course of 2007

TWEEDDALE

District Organiser: **Mrs Georgina Seymour,** Stobo Home Farm., Peebles EH45 8NX

Area Organisers: **Mrs D Balfour-Scott,** Dreva Craig, Broughton, Biggar ML12 6HH
       Mr K St. C Cunningham, Hallmanor, Peebles EH45 9JN
       Mrs H B Marshall, Baddinsgill, West Linton, EH46 7HL

Treasurer: **Mr Julian Birchall,** Drumelzier Old Manse, Biggar ML12 6JD

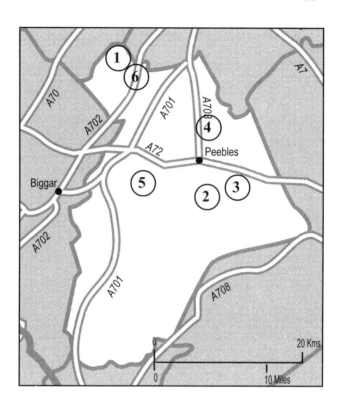

DATES OF OPENING

Kailzie Gardens, Peebles .... All year		10am - 5.30pm
Portmore, Eddleston .... June, July, Aug. by appt. Tel. 01721 730383		
Baddinsgill, West Linton .... Sunday 27 May		2 - 5pm
Hallmanor, Peebles .... Sunday 3 June		2 - 5.30pm
West Linton Village Gardens. .... Sunday 22 July		2 - 5pm
Portmore, Eddleston .... Sunday 29 July		2 - 5pm
Stobo Water Garden, Stobo, Peebles .... Sunday 21 October		12.30 - 4pm

1. BADDINSGILL, West Linton EH46 7HL

(Gavin and Elaine Marshall)

Beautiful woodland garden 1,000 ft up in the Pentland Hills above West Linton. Stunning situation. Woodland and riverside walks. Bluebells, azaleas and rhododendrons. Water garden.

Route: A702 to West Linton uphill past golf course.

Admission £3.50 Children free

SUNDAY 27 MAY 2 - 5pm

40% to Multiple Sclerosis Society Scotland   60% net to SGS Charities

&. (limited access)

2. HALLMANOR, Kirkton Manor, Peebles EH45 9JN

(Mr & Mrs K St C Cunningham)

Rhododendrons and azaleas, wooded grounds with loch and salmon ladder. Set in one of the most beautiful valleys in the Borders.

Route: Peebles 6 miles. Off A72 Peebles/Glasgow road. Follow SGS signs.

Admission £3.50 Children free

SUNDAY 3 JUNE 2 - 5.30pm

40% to Manor & Lyne Church   60% net to SGS Charities

&. (partially)

3. KAILZIE GARDENS, Peebles EH45 9HT

(Lady Buchan-Hepburn)

Semi-formal walled garden with shrub and herbaceous borders. Rose garden. Well stocked greenhouse. Woodland and burnside walks among massed spring bulbs, rhododendrons and azaleas. The garden is set among fine old trees and includes the old larch planted in 1724.

Route: $2^{1}/_{2}$ miles east of Peebles on B7062

ALL YEAR ROUND 10am - 5.30pm

Admission:

Mid March - 31 May	Adults £3.50 Children £1.00 Concessions £3.00
1 June - 31 October	Adults £4.50 Children £1.00 Concessions £3.50
1 November - mid March	Adults £2.00 Children under 5 free

40% Donation to Scotland's Gardens Scheme

&. (tearoom/licensed restaurant) Picnic area, children's play area, shop, 18 hole putting green, stocked trout pools. Visit the 'Osprey Watch' live CCTV beamed to a visitor centre

4. PORTMORE, Eddleston EH45 8QU

(Mr & Mrs David Reid)

Lovingly created by current owners over the past 20 years the gardens surrounding the David Bryce mansion house contain mature trees and offer fine views of the surrounding countryside. Large walled garden consists of box edged herbaceous borders planted in stunning colour harmonies, potager, rose garden pleached lime walk and ornamental fruit cages. The Victorian glasshouses contain fruit trees, roses, geraniums, pelargoniums and a wide variety of tender plants. Italianate Grotto. Recently developed water garden with shrubs and meconopsis. Woodland walks lined with rhododendrons, azaleas and shrub roses. Starred in 'Good Gardens Guide'

Route: of A703 1 mile north of Eddleston. Bus no. 62

Admission £4.00

SUNDAY 29 JULY 2 - 5pm

Also June, July and August by appointment Tel. 01721 730383

40% to Crossroads 60% net to SGS Charities

&. (partially) ⚞ ❀ (home grown) ☕ (cream)

5. STOBO WATER GARDEN, Stobo, Peebles EH45 8NX

(Mr & Mrs Hugh Seymour)

Garden was originally laid out about 100 years ago and features magnificent trees and shrubs; splendid waterfall; a side burn as well as a main stream crossed in several places by stepping stones. In the autumn the maples and acers turning vivid colours reflect in the pools. The cercidiphyllum scents the air with the aroma of burnt sugar. The lake at the top end of the garden is surrounded with splendid trees and rhododendrons. Sensible footwear.

Route: Peebles 7 miles, signposted on B712 Lyne/Broughton Road.

Admission £3.50 Children free.

SUNDAY 21 OCTOBER 12.30 - 4pm

40% to Marie Curie Cancer Care 60% net to SGS Charities

⚞ ☕

6. WEST LINTON VILLAGE GARDENS EH46 7DZ

A wonderful group: an upland garden, plantsman's gardens, cottage garden and a totally eco-friendly garden developed on sustainability and labour lightening methods by West Linton's answer to Bob Flowerdew. Wonderful woodland and herbaceous perennials, vegetables, herbs, shrubs.

Route: A701 0r A702 and follow signs.

Admission £4.00 includes all gardens. Children free. Tickets & maps in New Church Hall in centre of the village.

SUNDAY 22 JULY 2 - 5pm

40% to Ben Walton Trust 60% net to SGS Charities

&. (partially) ☕ (in New Church Hall) ❀ (in New Church Hall)

WIGTOWN

District Organiser: **Mrs Francis Brewis,** Ardwell House, Stranraer DG9 9LY

Area Organisers: **Mrs V Wolseley Brinton,** Chlenry, Castle Kennedy, Stranraer DG9 8SL
Mrs Andrew Gladstone, Craichlaw, Kirkcowan, Newton Stewart DG8 0DQ

Treasurer: **Mr G Fleming,** Ardgour, Stoneykirk, Stranraer DG9 9DL

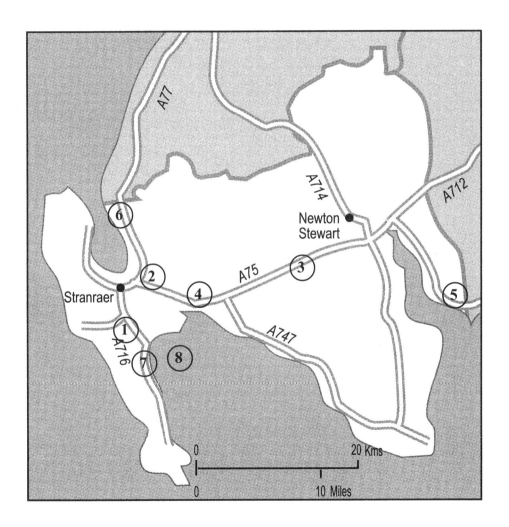

DATES OF OPENING

Ardwell House Gardens, Ardwell	1 April - 30 September daily	10am - 5pm
Castle Kennedy & Lochinch, Stranraer	1 April - 30 September daily	10am - 5pm
Glenwhan Gardens, by Stranraer	1 April - 31 October daily	10am - 5pm
Logan House Gardens, Port Logan	2 February - 1 April daily	10am - 4pm
	2 April - 31 August daily	9am - 6pm
Woodfall Gardens, Glasserton	May - 31 Aug. by appt.	Tel. 01988 500692

Kirkdale, Carsluith	Sunday 11 February	2 - 5pm
Kirkdale, Carsluith	Sunday 18 February	2 - 5pm
Logan House Gardens, Port Logan	Sunday 6 May	9am - 6pm
Lochryan House, Cairnryan	Sunday 20 May	2 - 5pm
Logan Botanic Garden, Port Logan	Sunday 27 May	10am - 6pm
Woodfall Gardens, Glasserton	Sunday 10 June	2 - 5.30pm
Glenwhan Gardens, by Stranraer	Sunday 24 June	10am - 5pm
Craichlaw, Kirkcowan	Sunday 1 July	2 - 5pm
Castle Kennedy & Lochinch Gardens, Stranraer	Sunday 8 July	10 - 5pm
Woodfall Gardens, Glasserton	Sunday 22 July	2 - 5.30pm

1. ARDWELL HOUSE GARDENS, Ardwell, Stranraer DG9 9LY
(Mr & Mrs Francis Brewis)
Daffodils, spring flowers, rhododendrons, flowering shrubs, coloured foliage and rock plants. Moist garden at smaller pond and a walk round larger ponds, with views over Luce Bay. Collecting box. House not open.
Route: A76 towards Mull of Galloway. Stranraer 10 miles.
Admission £3.00 Concessions £2.00 Children under 14 free
1 APRIL - 30 SEPTEMBER DAILY 10am - 5pm
Donation to Scotland's Gardens Scheme

 (and self-pick fruit in season) Picnic site on shore

2. CASTLE KENNEDY AND LOCHINCH GARDENS, Stranraer DG9 8RT **NEW**
(The Earl & Countess of Stair)
Located in beautiful scenery between two large natural lochs, the Gardens extend to seventy-five acres of landscaped terraces and avenues. With the romantic, ruined 16th Century Castle Kennedy overlooking a walled garden, at one end, and Lochinch Castle at the other, these famous gardens are unquely outstanding. In close proximity to the sea, the Gardens are greatly influenced by the Gulf Stream and contain many fine specimen trees, rhododendrons and tender exotic plants. Designed in 1722 by the 2nd Earl of Stair, Amabassador to France, who was greatly influenced by the gardens of Versailles, four carefully planned walks have been designed for visitors. These reveal the full garden experience throughout the seasons including the beautiful herbaceous border and woodland and loch-side walks.
Route: 5 miles from Stranraer on A75
Admission £4.00 OAP's £3.00 Children £1.00
4 FEBRUARY - 11 MARCH SUNDAYS 10am - 5pm
SUNDAY 8 JULY 10am - 5pm
Also 1 April - 30 September daily 10am - 5pm
40% to Homestart 60% net to SGS Charities

 (partly) Snowdrop talks and garden tours in February

3. CRAICHLAW, Kirkcowan DG8 0DQ
(Mr & Mrs Andrew Gladstone)
Formal garden around the house, with herbaceous borders. Set in extensive grounds with lawns, lochs and woodland. A path around the main loch leads to a water garden returning past an orchard of old Scottish apple varieties.
<u>Route:</u> signposted off A75, 8 miles west of Newton Stewart and B733, one mile west of Kirkcowan.
<u>Admission</u> £2.50 Accompanied children under 14 free
SUNDAY 1 JULY 2 - 5pm
40% to Kirkcowan Parish Church 60% net to SGS Charities

---

4. GLENWHAN GARDENS, by Stranraer DG9 8PH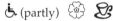
(Mr & Mrs W Knott)
Glenwhan Garden has been described as one of the best newly created gardens in recent times. It was hewn 20 years ago from a hillside covered in bracken and gorse. Two lochans from which there are magnificent views across Luce Bay were made by damming up bogs and provide a rich habitat for rare species. There are winding paths with rhododendrons, azaleas, shrub roses a primula area and a wooded streamside walk. This is a garden for all season, and there is something to discover at any time of the year, including red squirrels.
<u>Route:</u> 7 miles east of Stranraer, 1 mile off the A75 at Dunragit (follow signs)
<u>Admission</u> £4.00 OAP's £3.00 Children £1.50 Families £8.50
SUNDAY 24 JUNE 10am - 5pm
Also 1 April - 31 October daily 10am - 5pm
20% Amnesty International 20% Red Squirrel Trust 60% net to SGS Charities

---

5. KIRKDALE, Carsluith DG8 7EA
(Professor and Mrs David Hannay)
Woodland snowdrop walks round historic 18th Century property. A chance to view the only working water driven sawmill in South of Scotland and nature trail.
<u>Route:</u> 6 miles west of Gatehouse of Fleet on A75 signposted Cairnholy Chambered Cairn.
<u>Admission</u> £3.00 Children free
SUNDAY 11 FEBRUARY 2 - 5pm
SUNDAY 18 FEBRUARY 2 - 5pm
40% Creetown Silver Band 60% net to SGS Charities

 Snowdrops for sale, Working water-driven sawmill

---

5. LOCHRYAN HOUSE, Stranraer DG9 8QY
(Mr & Mrs Malcolm Wallace)
The garden behind the white-painted 18th Century Lochryan House retain the main elements of the original 18th Century layout. The central avenue leads to a transverse terraced bank with pavilions at either end. There are rhododendrons, flowering shrubs and some impressive trees to be admired.
<u>Route:</u> off A77 immediately north of Cairnryan Village.
<u>Admission</u> £2.50 Accompanied children under 14 free
SUNDAY 20 MAY 2 - 5pm
40% Marie Curie 60% net to SGS Charities

---

7. LOGAN BOTANIC GARDEN, Port Logan, by Stranraer DG8 8LY

(Regional Garden of the Royal Botanic Garden Edinburgh and one of the National Botanic Gardens of Scotland)

At the south-western tip of Scotland lies Logan which is unrivalled as the county's most exotic garden. With a mild climate washed by the Gulf Stream, a remarkable collection of bizarre and beautiful plants, especially from the southern hemisphere, flourish out-of-doors. Enjoy the colourful walled garden with its magnificent tree ferns, palms and borders and the contrasting woodland garden with its unworldly gunnera bog. Explore the Discovery Centre or take an audio tour.

Route: 10 miles south of Stranraer on A716, then 2½ miles from Ardwell village.
Admission £3.50 Concessions £3.00 Children £1.00 Family £8.00
SUNDAY 27 MAY 10am - 6pm
40% to Royal Botanic Garden Edinburgh 60% net to SGS Charities

 Home baking and botanic shop, Discovery Centre, guided tours

8. LOGAN HOUSE GARDENS, Port Logan, by Stranraer DG9 9ND

(Mr & Mrs Roberts)

Queen Anne house, 1701. Rare exotic tropical plants and shrubs. Fine species and hybrid rhododendrons.

Route: 14 miles south of Stranraer on A716, 2½ miles from Ardwell village.
Admission £3.00 Children under 16 Free
SUNDAY 6 MAY 9am -6pm
2 February - 1 April 10am - 4pm and 2 ApriL- 31 August Daily 9am - 6pm
40% to Port Logan Hall Fund 60% net to SGS Charities

9. WOODFALL GARDENS, Glasserton DG8 8LY

(David and Lesley Roberts)

A 3 acre 18th Century walled garden undergoing revitalisation. As well as the remains of the original garden buildings there are mixed borders, a woodland area, a parterre and a productive potager.

Route: 2 miles south of Whithorn by junction off A746/747
Admission Adults £2.50 Concessions £2.00 Accompanied children under 14 free
SUNDAY 10 JUNE 2 - 5.30pm
SUNDAY 22 JULY 2 - 5.30pm
May - end August by prior appointment 01988 500692
June Opening - 30% to the Swallow Theatre 10% to Glasserton and Isle of Whithorn Church 60% net to SGS Charities
July Opening - 30% Alzheimers (Scotland) 10% to Glasserton and Isle of Whithorn Church 60% net to SGS Charities

♿ ❉

July opening only The Swallow Theatre will provide an entertainment at 4pm (weather permitting).

153

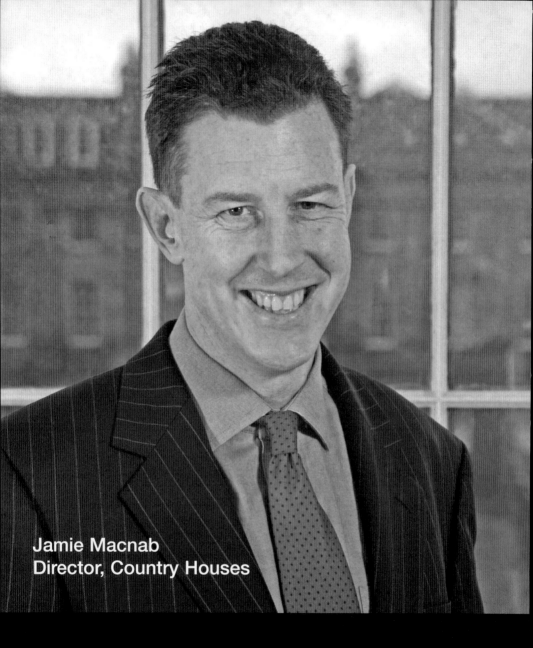

Jamie Macnab
Director, Country Houses

AUSTRALIA'S OPEN GARDEN SCHEME

AROUND 700 inspiring private gardens drawn from every Australian state and territory feature in our annual program.

Included are tropical gardens in the Northern Territory and Queensland, awe-inspiring arid zone gardens, traditional gardens in the temperate south, gardens which feature Australia's unique flora, and gardens designed by many of Australia's contemporary designers.

Our full colour guidebook is published each August by ABC Books and every entry includes a full description, map references and directions, opening details and amenities.

State-by-state calendars make it easy to plan a personal itinerary, and a special index identifies gardens with a particular plant collection or area of interest.

Also included are exhaustive listings of regularly open gardens around the country.

PRESIDENT: *Mrs Malcolm Fraser*
CHIEF EXECUTIVE OFFICER: *Neil Robertson*
Westport, New Gisborne, Victoria 3438
Tel +61 3 5428 4557
Fax +61 3 5428 4558
email: national@opengarden.org.au
website: www.opengarden.org.au
Australia's Open Garden Scheme ABN 60 057 467 553

ABC
BOOKS

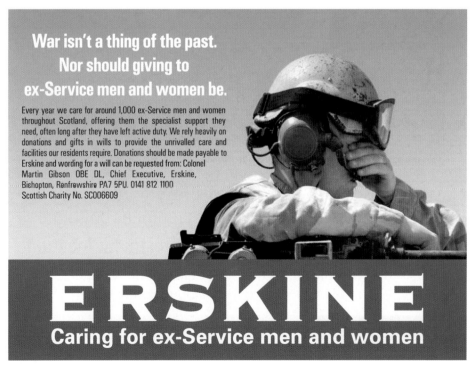

Charlotte
SQUARE

Charlotte Square

The Newest Investment Management boutique
in Scotland's oldest and finest investment location.

Contact William Forsyth: 43 Charlotte Square, Edinburgh EH2 4HQ
Tel: 0131 624 7709 www.charlotte-square.com

160

The National Trust
for Scotland

*Whatever the season,
the National Trust for Scotland's
gardens provide a place for colour,
variety, inspiration and enjoyment
- a place for everyone.*

Threave

Dumfries & Galloway

Broughton House and Garden

Off A711/A755, at 12 High Street, Kirkcudbright

A fascinating 18th-century house in a delightful harbour town, this was the home and studio from 1901 to 1933 of the artist E A Hornel, one of the 'Glasgow Boys'. His studio overlooks the one-acre Japanese-style garden he designed after visits to the Far East.

OPEN: *GARDEN: 1 Feb to 30 Mar, Mon-Fri 11-4. HOUSE AND GARDEN: 31 Mar to 30 June, Thurs-Mon, 12-5; 1 Jul to 30 Aug, daily 12-5; 1 Sept to 31 Oct, Thurs-Mon, 12-5.*

Adult	Family	1 Parent	Concession
£8	£20	£16	£5

Threave Garden, House and Estate

Off A75, 1m west of Castle Douglas

Best known for its spectacular daffodils, Threave is also a garden for all seasons, with bright herbaceous beds in summer, and vibrant trees and heather garden in autumn. The Victorian House, now open to visitors, is also home to the Trust's School of Practical Gardening. Visitor Centre with exhibition, shop and licensed restaurant; plant sales, guided walks.

OPEN: *VISITOR AND COUNTRYSIDE CENTRES, GIFT SHOP, PLANT CENTRE AND EXHIBITION ROOM: 1 Feb to 31 Mar, daily 10-4; 1 Apr to 31 Oct, daily 9.30-5.30; 1 Nov to 23 Dec, daily 10-4. RESTAURANT: 1 Feb to 31 Mar, daily 10-4; 1 Apr to 31 Oct, daily 10-5; 1 Nov to 23 Dec, daily 10-4. HOUSE: 1 Apr to 31 Oct, Wed, Thurs, Fri & Sun, 11-3.30. WALLED GARDEN & GLASSHOUSES: all year, daily 9.30-5 (9.30-4.30 Fri). GARDEN AND ESTATE: all year, daily.*

Adult	Family	1 Parent	Concession
£10	£25	£20	£7

Scottish Borders

Harmony Garden

In Melrose, opposite the Abbey

Wander through this tranquil garden's herbaceous borders, lawns and fruit and vegetable plots, and enjoy fine views of the Abbey and Eildon Hills.

OPEN: *31 Mar to 31 Oct, Mon-Sat 10-5, Sun 1-5.*

Adult	Family	1 Parent	Concession
£3	£8	£6	£2

Priorwood Gift Shop & Garden

In Melrose, beside the Abbey

Overlooked by the Abbey ruins, this unique garden produces plants for a superb variety of dried flower arrangements, made and sold here. The orchard contains many historic apple varieties.

OPEN: *GIFT SHOP: 5 Jan to 31 Mar, Mon-Sat 12-4; 1 Apr to 24 Dec, Mon-Sat 10-5, Sun 1-5. GARDEN: 31 Mar to 24 Dec, same opening times as shop*

Adult	Family	1 Parent	Concession
£3	£8	£6	£2

Ayrshire and Arran

Brodick Castle

Isle of Arran. Ferry: Ardrossan to Brodick (55 mins) connecting bus to Reception Centre (2m). Ferry between Claonaig and Lochranza (north Arran), frequent in summer, limited in winter; tel Caledonian MacBrayne. All-inclusive travel and admission ticket from Strathclyde Passenger Transport Stations (0870) 608 2608.

Built on the site of a Viking fortress and partly dating from the 13th century, this magnificent castle overlooks Brodick Bay and has as a backdrop the majestic Goatfell mountain range. The woodland garden, specialising in rhododendrons, is one of Europe's finest, where plants from the Himalayas, Burma and China flourish. Licensed restaurant, gift shop, plant sales, guided walks.

OPEN: *CASTLE: 30 March to 31 Oct, daily 11-4.30 (closes 3.30 in Oct).*

COUNTRY PARK: all year, daily 9.30-sunset.

RECEPTION CENTRE, SHOP AND WALLED GARDEN: 30 March to 31 Oct, daily 10-4.30, 1

Greenbank Garden

Nov to 21 Dec, Fri/Sat/Sun 10-3.30.

RESTAURANT: 30 March to 31 Oct, daily 11-5

Adult	Family	1 Parent	Concession
£10	£25	£20	£7

Culzean Castle and Country Park

12m south of Ayr, on A719, 4m west of Maybole, off A77

One of Scotland's major attractions – a perfect day out for all the family. Robert Adam's romantic 18th-century masterpiece is perched on a cliff high above the Firth of Clyde. The Fountain Garden lies in front of the castle with terraces and herbaceous borders reflecting its Georgian elegance.

The extensive country park offers beaches and rockpools, parklands, gardens, woodland walks and adventure playground. It contains fascinating restored buildings contemporary with the castle. Visitor Centre, shops, plant sales, restaurants and exhibitions. Ranger service events and guided walks.

OPEN: *CASTLE AND WALLED GARDEN: 30 March to 31 Oct, daily 10.30-5 (last entry 4).*

COUNTRY PARK: all year, daily 9.30-sunset.

VISITOR CENTRE: 30 March to 31 Oct, daily 9.30-5.30; 1 Nov to 29 March, Thu/Fri/Sat/Sun 11-4

OTHER VISITOR FACILITIES: 30 March to 31 Oct, daily 10.30-5.30.

Adult	Family	1 Parent	Concession
£12	£30	£25	£8

Greater Glasgow

Geilston Garden

On the A814 at west end of Cardross, 18m north-west of Glasgow

A delightful garden, laid out over 200 years ago, and retaining a sense of private space into which the visitor is invited. Attractive features include a walled garden and a burn, winding through the wooded glen.

OPEN: *30 March to 31 Oct, daily 9.30-5.*

Adult	Family	1 Parent	Concession
£5	£14	£10	£4

Greenbank Garden

Flenders Road, off Mearns Road, Clarkston. Off M77 and A726, 6m south of Glasgow city centre

A unique walled garden with plants and designs of particular interest to suburban gardeners. Fountains, woodland walk and special area for disabled visitors. Shop, plant sales, and gardening demonstrations throughout the year.

OPEN: *GARDEN: all year, daily 9.30-sunset.*

SHOP AND TEAROOM: 30 March to 31 Oct, daily 11-5; 1 Nov to 29 March, Sat/Sun 2-4.

HOUSE: 30 March to 31 Oct, Sun 2-4.

Adult	Family	1 Parent	Concession
£5	£14	£10	£4

Lothians and Fife

Inveresk Lodge Garden

A6124, near Musselburgh, 6m east of Edinburgh

This sunny hillside garden in the historic village of Inveresk entices visitors with its colourful herbaceous beds, attractive shrubs and old roses selected by Graham Stuart Thomas. Restored Edwardian conservatory with aviary.

OPEN: *All year, daily 10-6 or dusk if earlier.*

Adult	Family	1 Parent	Concession
£3	£8	£6	£2

Malleny Garden

Off the A70, in Balerno, 6m west of Edinburgh city centre

A peaceful walled garden with a collection of old-fashioned roses and fine herbaceous borders. Special features are the 400-year-old clipped yew trees.

OPEN: *All year, daily 10-6 or dusk if earlier.*

Adult	Family	1 Parent	Concession
£3	£8	£6	£2

Malleny Garden

Culross

Off A985, 12m west of Forth Road Bridge and 4m east of Kincardine Bridge, Fife

Relive the domestic life of the 16th and 17th centuries amid the old buildings and cobbled streets of this Royal Burgh on the River Forth. A model 17th-century garden has been recreated behind Culross Palace to show the range of plants available and includes vegetables, culinary and medicinal herbs, soft fruits and ornamental shrubs. Shop and tearoom.

OPEN: *PALACE, STUDY, TOWN HOUSE AND BESSIE BAR TEAROOM: 31 March to 31 May, Thur-Mon 12-5; 1 Jun to 31 Aug, daily 12-5; 1 to 30 Sep, Thur-Mon 12-5; 1 to 31 Oct, Thur-Mon 12-4. GARDEN: all year, daily 10-6 or sunset if earlier.*

Adult	Family	1 Parent	Concession
£5	£14	£10	£4

Falkland Palace, Garden and Town Hall

A912, 11m north of Kirkcaldy. 10m from M90, junction 8

Set in a medieval village, the Royal Palace of Falkland is a superb example of Renaissance architecture. The stunning gardens were restored to a design by Percy Cane and give a long-lasting display — from spring-flowering cherry trees to the rich autumn colouring of maples. Exhibition and gift shop.

OPEN: *PALACE & GARDEN: 1 March to 31 Oct, Mon-Sat 10-5, Sun 1-5. GIFT SHOP: 1 March to 31 Oct, Mon-Sat 10-5; Sun 1-5; 1 Nov to 23 Dec and 5 Jan to 29 Feb, Mon-Sat 11-4, Sun 1-4.*

Adult	Family	1 Parent	Concession
£8	£20	£16	£5

Hill of Tarvit

Off A916, 2m south of Cupar

This fine house and garden were rebuilt in 1906 by the renowned Scottish architect Sir Robert Lorimer, for a Dundee industrialist, whose superb collection of furniture is on view. Visitors can wander through the fragrant walled garden, linger on the terraces or enjoy the heady scent of roses in the sunken garden. Shop and tearoom.

OPEN: *31 March to 31 May, Thur-Mon 1-5 (tearoom & shop open 12); 1 Jun to 31 Aug, daily 1-5 (tearoom & shop open 12); 1 to 30 Sep, Thur-Mon 1-5 (tearoom & shop open 12); 1 to 31 Oct, Thur-Mon 1-4 (tearoom & shop open 12) .*

Adult	Family	1 Parent	Concession
£8	£20	£16	£5

Kellie Castle and Garden

On B9171, 3m north of Pittenweem

This superb castle dates from the 14th century and was sympathetically restored by the Lorimer family in the late 19th century. The late Victorian garden has a selection of old-fashioned roses and herbaceous plants, cultivated organically. Shop and tearoom.

OPEN: *CASTLE: 31 March to 31 Oct, daily 1-5 (tearoom & shop open 12). GARDEN: all year, daily 9.30-5.30. Estate: all year, daily.*

Adult	Family	1 Parent	Concession
£8	£20	£16	£5

Perthshire and Angus

Branklyn Garden

116 Dundee Road, Perth

This attractive garden was first established in 1922. It contains outstanding collections of rhododendrons, alpines, herbaceous and peat-garden plants and is particularly famed for its

Azaleas at Branklyn Garden

Meconopsis and its autumn colour.

OPEN: *GARDEN AND SHOP: 31 March to 31 Oct, daily 10-5. Shop opening times may vary.*

Adult	Family	1 Parent	Concession
£5	£14	£10	£4

House of Dun

3 miles west of Montrose on the A935

This beautiful house, overlooking the Montrose Basin, was designed by William Adam in 1730. The restored walled garden displays period herbaceous and rose borders. Shop, restaurant, woodland walks.

OPEN: *HOUSE: 31 March to 30 Jun, Wed-Sun (closed Mon and Tue), 12.30-5.30; 1 Jul to 31 Aug, daily 11.30-5.30; 1 Sep to 31 Oct, Wed-Sun (closed Mon and Tue), 12.30-5.30 (last admission 45 mins before closing). Guided tours only. GARDEN: all year, daily 9-sunset. Grounds: all year, daily. Property will open on Bank Holiday weekends from Friday to Monday inclusive.*

Adult	Family	1 Parent	Concession
£8	£20	£16	£5

Aberdeen and Grampian

Castle Fraser and Garden

Off A944, 4m north of Dunecht and 16m west of Aberdeen

One of the grandest Castles of Mar, this magnificent building was completed in 1636 by two master mason families. Walled garden, woodland walks, plant sales, adventure playground, courtyard café and shop.

OPEN: *CASTLE: 31 March to 30 Jun, Wed-Sun (closed Mon and Tue) 11-5; 1 Jul to 31 Aug, daily 11-5; 1 Sep to 31 Oct, Wed-Sun (closed Mon and Tue) 12-5 (last admission 45 mins before closing). SHOP: same times as castle and also open 3 Nov to*

16 Dec, Sat/Sun 12-4. GARDENS AND GROUNDS: all year, daily. Property will be open on Bank Holiday weekends from Friday to Monday inclusive.

Adult	Family	1 Parent	Concession
£8	£20	£16	£5

Crathes Castle, Garden and Estate

On A93, 3m east of Banchory and 15m west of Aberdeen

Turrets, gargoyles and superb original painted ceilings are features of this enchanting castle, built in the late 16th century. The eight gardens within the walled garden provide a wonderful display all year round. Visitor Centre, restaurant, shop and plant sales, exciting trails and an adventure playground.

OPEN: *CASTLE: 31 March to 30 Sep, daily 10.30-5.30, 1 to 31 Oct, daily 10.30-4.30; 1 Nov to 31 March, Wed-Sun (closed Mon and Tue) 10.30-3.45. Last admission 45 mins before closing.*

PLANT SALES: same dates, but weekends only in Oct and closed Nov to March inclusive.

GARDENS: all year, daily 9-sunset. GROUNDS: ALL YEAR, daily. SKYTREK AERIAL TREKKING COURSE: contact property for details.

SHOP AND CATERING: 31 March to 31 Oct, daily 10-5.30; 1 Nov to 31 March, daily 10-4.30. Castle, restaurant and shop closed for Christmas and New Year holidays.

Adult	Family	1 Parent	Concession
£10	£25	£20	£7

Drum Castle and Garden

Off A93, 3m west of Peterculter, 8m east of Banchory and 10m west of Aberdeen

The late 13th-century keep, fine adjoining Jacobean mansion house and the additions of Victorian lairds make Drum unique. The Garden of Historic Roses represents different periods of gardening from the 17th to the 20th centuries. Woodland trails, children's playground, shop and tearoom.

OPEN: *CASTLE: 31 March to 30 Jun, daily (but closed Tue and Fri), 12.30-5; 1 Jul to 31 Aug, daily 11-5; 1 Sep to 31 Oct, daily (but closed Tue and Fri), 12.30-5. Last admission 45 mins before closing. GARDEN OF HISTORIC ROSES: 31 March to 31 Oct, daily 10-6. Grounds: all year, daily. Property will open on Bank Holiday weekends from Friday to Monday inclusive.*

Adult	Family	1 Parent	Concession
£8	£20	£16	£5

Pitmedden Garden

Arduaine Garden

Fyvie Castle

Off A947, 8m south-east of Turriff and 25m north of Aberdeen

The charm of Fyvie ranges from its 13th-century origins to its opulent Edwardian interiors. Superb collection of arms and armour and paintings, including works by Raeburn and Gainsborough. Stroll around the picturesque lake, or visit the restored 1903 racquet court and bowling alley. Shop and tearoom.

OPEN: *CASTLE: 31 March to 30 Jun, Sat-Wed (closed Thur & Fri) 12-5; 1 Jul to 31 Aug, daily 11-5; 1 Sep to 31 Oct, Sat-Wed (closed Thur and Fri) 12-5 (last admission 4.15). GARDEN: all year, daily 9-sunset.*

GROUNDS: all year, daily. Property will open on Bank Holiday weekends from Friday to Monday inclusive.

Adult	Family	1 Parent	Concession
£8	£20	£16	£5

Haddo House

Off B999, near Tarves, 19m north of Aberdeen

This elegant mansion house boasts sumptuous Victorian interiors beneath a crisp Georgian exterior. Noted for fine furniture and paintings, Haddo also has a delightful terrace garden, leading to a Country Park with lakes, walks and monuments. Shop, plant sales and restaurant.

OPEN: *HOUSE: 31 March to 30 Jun, Fri-Mon 11-5; 1 Jul to 31 Aug, daily 11-5; 1 Sep to first weekend in Nov, Fri-Mon 11-5 (last admission to house 4.15). Guided tours only. GARDEN: all year, daily 9-sunset. GROUNDS: all year, daily.*

Adult	Family	1 Parent	Concession
£8	£20	£16	£5

Leith Hall and Garden

On B9002, 1m west of Kennethmont and 34m north-west of Aberdeen

This mansion house was the home for almost 300 years of the Leith family, and the elegantly furnished rooms reflect their lifestyle. Outside, wander among the glorious herbaceous borders or explore the estate trails. Picnic area and tearoom.

OPEN: *HOUSE AND TEAROOM: 31 March to 30 Jun, weekends only 12-5; 1 Jul to 31 Aug, daily 12-5; 1 Sep to 31 Oct, weekends only 12-5 (last admission 4.15).*

GARDEN: all year, daily 9-sunset.

GROUNDS: all year, daily. Property will open on Bank Holiday weekends from Friday to Monday inclusive. .

Adult	Family	1 Parent	Concession
£8	£20	£16	£5

Pitmedden Garden

On A920, 1m west of Pitmedden village and 14m north of Aberdeen

In the Great Garden, the elaborate original parterre designs of the 17th century have been carefully re-created and are spectacularly filled in summer with some 40,000 annual flowers. Picnic area, shop, tearoom.

OPEN: *GARDEN, MUSEUM OF FARMING LIFE, SHOP AND TEAROOM: 1 May to 30 Sep, daily 10-5.30 (last admission 5).*

GROUNDS: all year, daily.

Adult	Family	1 Parent	Concession
£5	£14	£10	£4

Highlands

Arduaine Garden

On A816, 20m south of Oban and 18m north of Lochgilphead

Arduaine boasts spectacular rhododendrons and azaleas in late spring and early summer, but its perennial borders are magnificent throughout the season. Stroll through the woodland to the

Crarae Garden

Inverewe Garden

coastal viewpoint, or relax in the water garden.

OPEN: *GARDEN: all year, daily 9.30-sunset. RECEPTION CENTRE: 30 March to 30 Sep, daily 9.30-4.30 .*

Adult	Family	1 Parent	Concession
£5	£14	£10	£4

Balmacara Estate and Lochalsh Woodland Garden

A87, 3m east of Kyle of Lochalsh

A crofting estate of 6,795 acres with superb views of Skye and Applecross. Lochalsh Woodland Garden enjoys a tranquil setting by the shore of Loch Alsh and has a collection of hardy ferns, fuchsias, hydrangeas, bamboos and rhododendrons.

OPEN: *RECEPTION KIOSK: 31 March to 30 Sep, daily 9-5. BALMACARA SQUARE VISITOR CENTRE: 31 March to 30 Sep, daily 9-5 (Fri 9-4). Estate: all year, daily. WOODLAND GARDEN: all year, daily 9-sunset.*

Pay and display £2

Brodie Castle

Off A96 4^1/$_2$m west of Forres and 24m east of Inverness

A 16th-century tower house with 17th- and 19th-century additions, Brodie has unusual plaster ceilings, a major art collection, porcelain and fine furniture. In springtime the grounds are carpeted with the daffodils for which the castle is rightly famous.

OPEN: *CASTLE: 31 March to 30 Apr, daily 10.30-5; 1 May to 30 Jun, Sun-Thur 10.30-5; 1 Jul to 31 Aug, daily 10.30-5; 1Sep to 31 Oct, Sun-Thur 10.30-5 (last tour starts 4.30). TEAROOM AND SHOP: 31 March to 30 Apr, daily 11-4; 1 May to 30 Jun, Sun-Thur 11-4; 1 Jul to 31 Aug, daily 11-4; 1 Sep to 31 Oct, Sun-Thur 11-4 (last entry to tearoom 4). GROUNDS: all year, daily.*

Adult	Family	1 Parent	Concession
£8	£20	£16	£5

Crarae Garden

A83, 10m south of Inveraray

Set on a hillside down which tumbles the Crarae Burn, this delightful garden is reminiscent of a Himalayan gorge. Tree and shrub collections are rich and diverse. The garden contains one of the best collections of the genus *Rhododendron* in Scotland, unusually rich in cultivars, as well as part of the National Collection of *Nothofagus* and particularly good representations of *Acer, Eucalyptus, Eucryphia* and *Sorbus.* The autumn colours of the leaves and berries are well worth a visit too. Plant sales, shop and tearoom.

OPEN: *VISITOR CENTRE: 30 March to 30 Sep, daily 10-5. Site: all year, daily 9.30-sunset*

Adult	Family	1 Parent	Concession
£5	£14	£10	£4

Inverewe Garden

On A832, by Poolewe, 6m north-east of Gairloch

The tallest Australian gum trees in Britain, sweet-scented Chinese rhododendrons, exotic trees from Chile and Blue Nile lilies from South Africa, all grow here in this spectacular lochside setting, favoured by the warm currents of the North Atlantic Drift. Visitor Centre, shop, plant sales, licensed restaurant.

OPEN: *GARDEN: 1 Jan to 30 March, daily 9.30-4; 31 Mar to 31 Oct, daily 9.30-9 or sunset if earlier.*

VISITOR CENTRE AND SHOP: 31 March to 30 Sep, daily 9.30-5; 1 to 31 Oct, daily 9.30-4.

RESTAURANT: 31 Mar to 30 Sep, daily 10-5; 1 to 31 Oct, daily 10-4. Additional opening may be introduced over winter months - please call for details.

Adult	Family	1 Parent	Concession
£8	£20	£16	£5

The National Trust
for Scotland

Plants for Sale!

*We hope you enjoy your visit to a magical National Trust for Scotland garden.
At some of our gardens we can offer you the perfect souvenir —
a chance to recreate a bit of that garden in your own garden.
We now sell plants from 17 of our garden properties as listed below:*

- **Falkland Palace**
- **Broughton House**
- **Greenbank Garden**
- **Inverewe Garden**
- **Pitmedden Garden**
- **Threave Garden**

- **Kellie Castle**
- **Hugh Miller Museum
  & Birthplace Cottage**
- **House of Dun**
- **Branklyn Garden**
- **Brodick Castle**

- **Castle Fraser**
- **Crathes Castle**
- **Culzean Castle**
- **Hill of Tarvit**
- **Crarae Garden**
- **Drum Castle**

*This varies from a few tables of our home grown plants at some properties,
to a full blown plant centre with a wide selection of shrubs, rhododendrons,
herbaceous plants, alpines and roses at others. Some of the plants
will have been grown in the garden.*

We are delighted to be able to offer plants like the famous Primula *'Inverewe'*
and Crocosmia *'Culzean Pink'. We also offer a wide selection of bulbs in
season and some of the gardens now produce their own packets of seed.*

*The next time you visit a National Trust for Scotland property look out
for the exciting range of garden plants on offer.*

*All the proceeds from the sales contribute to the vital
conservation work of the Trust.*

For more information please contact our properties directly.

Index to Advertisers

GARDENS OF SCOTLAND
2008

Order now and your copy will be posted to you on publication in February

Scotland's Gardens Scheme
42a Castle Street, Edinburgh EH2 3BN

Please send me_____ copy/copies of
"Gardens of Scotland 2008"
Price £6.50, to include p&p, as soon as it is available
I enclose a cheque/postal order made payable to
<u>Scotland's Gardens Scheme</u>

Name..

Address..

Postcode....................